Books by Harvey Havel:

Noble McCloud (1999)
The Imam (2000)
Freedom of Association (2006)
From Poets to Protagonists (2009)
Harvey Havel's Blog, Essays (2011)
Stories from the Fall of the Empire (2011)
Two Tickets to Memphis (2012)
Mother, A Memoir (2013)
Charlie Zero's Last-Ditch Attempt (2014)
The Orphan of Mecca, Book One (2016)
The Orphan of Mecca, Book Two (2016)
The Orphan of Mecca, Book Three (2016)
The Thruway Killers (2017)
Mister Big (2018)
The Wild Gypsy of Arbor Hill (2019)
A Rumination on the Role of Love during A
Condition of Extreme Conservatism and Extreme
Liberalism (2019)

A Rumination on The Role of Love During a Condition of Extreme Conservatism and Extreme Liberalism

A Political Essay

By

Harvey Havel

Because of the dynamic nature of the Internet, any web addresses or links contained in this book may have changed since publication and may no longer be valid. The views expressed in this work are solely those of the author and do not necessarily reflect the views of the publisher, and the publisher hereby disclaims any responsibility for them.

ISBN: 978-0-578-53686-6

For Dr. John Gillroy

Ecclesiastes --- כִּי לְכֶלֶב חַי הוּא טוֹב מִן הָאַרְיֵה הַמֵּת

*(And, also, for the members of the Beta-Beta Chapter
of that tiny college in Connecticut, with gratitude for
the education they freely gave me).*

Foreword

At my old college a long time ago, all of the professors there influenced me in some kind of way. There was Dr. Milla Riggio of the English department, a middle-aged and attractive professor whose lessons taught me the value of rigorously avoiding the glaring human cycle of revenge and how such cycles had to be broken.

When I enrolled in her class at the college, I went through a mental breakdown, and I visited Professor Riggio first. Her assistant, Margaret Grasso, also tried to help, but I wore on her patience after a short while, and so I stopped going to the English department to look for serious psychiatric and medical attention from the Professors there. There was also a younger Dr. Diane Hunter, a hard-edged feminist whose arguments were so clear, that one could cut diamonds from them. She was an intolerable bitch back then, but pound-for-pound, she was one of the best professors the college ever had. Now that she has retired, I wouldn't be surprised if she remains a much more conservative feminist who is loyal to her roots as an old-fashioned bra-burner.

Elizabeth Libbey comes to mind as well, especially when she figured out that I neither had little idea what creative writing was nor was I in the right class to begin with. She discovered that I had skipped over the required introductory writing course in English, because I had thought that I had spent all of my time writing only the most advanced, talented, and highly mature work that would have never passed for anything acceptable. Tea Eakins, another writing instructor, also tried to communicate with me and even help me through my difficulties, but she found me incredibly rebellious and uncommunicative when she tried to get to me know me.

And then I took a writing workshop with a wonderful spirit and fiction writer named Nancy Slonim Aronie. Her class so liberated all of us that it became the most influential class I had ever taken on the college grounds. There were even two younger students who began seeing each other seriously as a result of it.

It is also worth mentioning here that Nancy Slonim Aronie went so far as to recommend me to the same literary agent who represented her in her latest published project, an agent named Phillipa Brophy of Sterling Lord Literastic in New York. Ms. Brophy even wrote a personal note to me on her rejection letterhead that said that I couldn't use the word "insane" as some kind of monolithic word. And even though I believed myself going insane at the time, I had little or no idea then, as I know now, that going insane demands more specificity. It seemed "insane" was the only reasonable

4

explanation I could find for whatever I had been feeling. Several years later I finally discovered there were libraries stocked with books by experts on what insanity meant. It turned out Ms. Brophy was right.

I had a wonderful Classics professor, named John C. Williams, who taught me how to write in a style that could be best described as sparse, forcible, direct, and impactful. He not only taught me about Homer, Virgil, Herodotus, and the human qualities of the Greek Gods, but I understand him now to have had, not only a brilliant mind, but also amazing pedagogy.

Professor Andrew Gold took an interest in me, and since he had served as my second-year advisor, my own psychiatrist father even met with him. Dr. Gold and my father had a good discussion, but in Southeast Asia, it is sometimes customary for a man to be so moved by a conversation, that he begins shaking his head in what looks like to be a fundamental disagreement. My father, after a short time with Dr. Gold, also shook his head, and the poor professor, thinking that my father disagreed with him on all of the feedback he gave about his son, had to stop and think of a good, logical argument to persuade him that he was right and that my father was terribly wrong. After a couple of years, I had heard that Dr. Gold was one of the toughest professors at the college, so I made sure to avoid his celebrity course on Constitutional Law. I'm still lucky to have avoided that course.

Professor Gold also gave me a wonderful economics textbook that I soon used on a semester abroad in England, but when I arrived at this school in London, the Economics professors there had changed their initial method of teaching and lecturing from the book. Dr. Gold had presented me with a book describing the basics of Economic Theory in the understandable words of English. When I had arrived at the school in England, though, as I sat in the same lecture hall as the same authors of this same book, they taught the students, in this gigantic sized and tremendously packed auditorium there, basic economic theories all in the pure language of Mathematics. Once again, I had no clue what I was doing. The professors who had originally written the book in plain English now spoke to the large audience of young people in Calculus.

Dr. Maurice Wade taught me the pleasures of reading philosophy, although we all sat in silence through his classes. I know now that he must have been bored silly by his inability to understand our shyness or the fact that we did not comprehend what he said to be close enough to pass his course. He gave most of us 'B's for our final grades. We deserved far worse. We were usually all hungover for most of the classes he tried so valiantly to teach.

Similarly, all of the students, instructors, and professors in the Math Department tried to teach me the basics of statistics, but I knew nothing then, and I still know nothing about the basic probable outcomes of dice now. I went to tutoring sessions, extra help sessions, and also met with a couple of Math professors several times, just to make sure I could grasp even the most basic problems of math and its terrible cohort, statistics. This did not work. I had no clue what I was doing then, and I still don't know anything about Statistics or Mathematics now. Because I'm so broke, I suddenly find myself learning Math at the local bodegas and convenience stores, albeit very slowly.

The professor whose Calculus class I took, by the way, also spoke in Calculus. From day one in Dr. Poliferno's class, I had no idea what he taught, and I did not know anything about basic Calculus by the class' end. There was a fellow student in the class who sat next to me, and I saw that he received an 'A' on his Calculus exam. I realized then that I wasn't exactly a Math person and that I had been foiled again.

And then out of the blue came a middle-aged, soft-spoken professor who challenged everyone in his class to learn the basics of political theory. The class at the time was a very small one. A handful of students, roughly three times a week, sat in silence, because they were either way too shy for such an environment or they understood the material completely enough that they didn't need to speak. The only one in the class who was challenged by the basics of political theory was I.

Because I was so challenged by, and because I had been an innocent dunderhead to begin with who had no idea or understanding of how or why such a college even let me in to begin with, I threw myself into study, determined to learn all aspects of political theory. After a few days, I became the only person in the small group to take over the class, and I explained everything I had learned from the textbooks and theories we read.

It began slowly, this ultimate rise to the top of the political science class, but once I was there, I basically became the only one in the class who discussed the books or talked at all. I had a mind that wouldn't stop, and a mouth that wouldn't stop talking. The other students had probably become so sick of me that they must have thought about dropping the course altogether. And when my mind operated so fiercely, I realize, now that I am approaching fifty-years old, that all I did was regurgitate the same information from those class textbooks over and over again. I just never intuitively grasped the material at all. I could have been giving some kind of poetry reading where I recited those lines directly from the page, almost pontificating them to the class, as though I finally understood something.

When I studied the infamous Prisoner's Dilemma, I didn't even get a good grade on our midterm exam, thinking that I had really made a breakthrough. The good professor had tested us about the preferences of each prisoner, and on the exam, I mistook the number '4' for being the lowest preference, and the number '1' for being the highest preference. It was actually the other way around. The directions said that '4' was the highest, and '1' was the lowest. I had written on the exam that I believed the Prisoner's Dilemma was some kind of difficult game of chicken with an insurance component. Naturally, when I came to the professor with the glitch, he smiled and said that I had been lobbying for my own interests, but he still kept my terrible grade intact.

Oddly enough, this middle-aged, somewhat soft-spoken professor took a kind of interest in me that I had never felt before. Like the other professors at the fair school, this political science professor was brilliant, and the students, bored and tired and very sick of me, also saw this brilliance. He would often get so excited about the subject matter at hand that it actually pleased him and even enthused him to continue his discussions and probe us with questions. I can safely say that this course had been the most challenging course I had ever taken anywhere, and it's also safe to say that this good professor should have brought a dunce hat to class for me to wear instead of letting me rule the classroom with my regurgitated breakthroughs in both academia and political theory. But he had always taken some sort of personal interest in me and hoped that I would one day follow in his footsteps, even though he may have wanted to do away with me altogether at the same time.

When this professor learned of my sudden and fortunate employment at *The CBS Evening News with Dan Rather* in nearby New York City, he took an even greater interest in me and never failed to tell his students about this accomplishment. In later years, after having held various entry-level jobs at *CBS News*, I must admit that I left the place, because I knew that I had been terribly incompetent in all aspects of television, radio, and print journalism and would soon be let go, because I never really understood the news business to begin with. After a few months there, I had to succumb to working the graveyard shift at *CBS News Radio*, because my performance was that bad as a humble, entry-level desk assistant. I now know that shy, sensitive, and passive people really don't belong in the news business.

And when I returned to school and faced this professor again long after my leave of absence from the college and after an initial internship with *CBS*, I found him looking at me from afar on the grounds of the college. When I spotted him, I even walked up to him and tried to say something. He could only look at me and grin warmly.

At the time, he must have known that I was having severe mental troubles. I wanted him to praise me again. I wanted him to say that I had been the most brilliant student in all of his political science classes combined. I wanted him to say that he would streamline my acceptance to the university he had once attended in Chicago. Instead, his lips were narrow, even though on the inside he again smiled. He said to me, "you've always been a good student." And then, after all that I had been through in nearby New York, my jaw almost dropped.

I guess I wanted him to say that my theories were as brilliant as Einstein's, John Nash's, or John Rawls'. And so, that was the last time I really ever saw him at the college. I did see him once again at a college play that the theater department had put on several months later, but at the time he sat with Dr. Wade far away, and I didn't want to disturb him. But that was about it. And now, he has disappeared, and now, as I approach the age of fifty, I don't even know how to locate him, where to send him a letter, or even know how to contact him through email.

I've tried contacting him, but like so many professors and teachers alike that we meet along the way of our tortuous journey through academia, he has disappeared, and I just can't seem to find him now. Since then, I have been all over the world. I have been to the top of the financial ladder, and now I sit at the very bottom. I have declared personal bankruptcy twice, I have been on at least a dozen psychiatric wards, and I have read so many books that I now tend to fall asleep after reading just the first few pages of one. I was even put in Albany County Jail for three drunken driving arrests. And now I am broke. Since I am beginning to put the recklessness of my past behind me, I am still trying to imagine what this amazing, helpful professor would say to me now. But if I were to have the privilege of talking to him today, wherever he lived or had lived, whether he had passed away or was still alive, whether or not he took good care of himself since the time I saw him, or even if he did not, I still know what he would say to me if we met.

He would give me a grin, and just maybe he would even smile. He would say what said to me many years ago. He would say, "you've always been a good student." And so, this work of what may be another one of my catastrophic plans to impress him, is dedicated to Professor John Gillroy, wherever he is, wherever he has gone, and wherever he may go.

Introduction

To begin any discussion of what such a rumination on a subject such as this entails, we must first make clear what the differences are between the political modes of thought that are summarized in this short essay.

While there are infinitely many political thoughts and theories that inhabit the wide political landscape of political belief, the two predominant ones that have survived within our democracy are the ideas of political conservatism and political liberalism.

Generally, political conservatives believe that the government that governs least is the best form of government, to paraphrase Theroux. Political conservatives believe in free market capitalism, low taxes, strong defense, the strong enforcement of contracts, fewer laws, local governance, decentralized power within a nation, rigorous market competition, strong families, the importance of religion and faith in daily life, and less regulation of industry. These are general characteristics, but many would agree that these are the major tenets of political conservatism. There are many other ideas and theories that add to this idea, and political opinions differ within the realm of political Conservativism, but these are the general pillars of the political conservative.

In terms of political theory, however, political Conservativism, while including libertarianism as well, relates mostly to the ideas and philosophies of classic liberalism, which is what is at the heart of what we have today in political Conservativism. The idea, in general terms, is that there should be more freedom within a society by fewer laws that govern its citizens, because citizens already have ethical and moral, built-in and more practical, and contractual incentives to behave in a law-abiding manner anyway. Add to this Adam Smith's theory that the 'invisible hand' of capitalism will eventually guide our nation towards increased prosperity, and thus, from this, we have in our democracy of today the entrenchment of political Conservativism. We have to note, however, that because the two terms, classic liberalism and political Conservativism, are used quite loosely in this essay, it is important that we don't confuse the two ideas.

Similarly, we also have to examine the idea of socialism as a theory as well as differentiate it from what has evolved from it. In terms of today's world within Western democracies, those who adhere to socialist principles, mainly the control and ownership of industry by the government, high regulation of industry, and the guarantee of the equality of all citizens, regardless of any differences in talents or materials or possessions, can be similar to the more moderate position of those in any given democracy as being politically liberal. So, if one is a socialist, one generally believes in a very strong government that protects its people from inequality, corporate corruption, and the abuse of power by the wealthy few. And here we have to differentiate the idea of socialism from its extreme cousin, which is the idea generally known as Communism or the theory of its foundation, known as Marxism or Leninism.

Communism builds on socialist ideas by championing labor within a society more than anything else. The ruling class in any Communist society is known as the proletariat, or the laboring class, that governs both industry and politics within its borders. A Communist government has a strong centralized government, ensures equality for all, guarantees labor, and simplifies economic outcomes by relying chiefly on a Marxist concept known as 'surplus value'. The former Soviet Union is the best example of what was an experiment of the first Communist nation.

But apart from this, and within the context of Western democracy, socialism has evolved into what we have now, which is political liberalism. Liberals within our nation also believe in the capitalist system of economy, but they generally believe that industry and corporations have to be regulated in order to protect citizens from abuse and corruption. Also, political liberals tend to believe in the idea that good government can act as a buffer to soften the inadequacies of both the democratic form of government as well as untethered market capitalism.

Political liberals believe in strong labor unions to protect the interests of workers, and they also insist on greater equality in the nation rather than the unbridled freedom that tends to bring inequality to its citizens. France may be an example of a politically liberal nation, although some may even tend to label France as a more socialist country, despite its democratic foundations. We must also say liberals believe in a more regulated type of economy that ensures the equal opportunity of all citizens, despite differences in class, race, and gender, to participate in its prosperity.

Now that we have outlined these distinctions as well as acknowledged that these terms will be used more loosely from this point forward, we can now ask the fundamental question that is the main subject of this essay. Can love exist within the paradigms of extreme political liberalism and extreme political conservatism? It is the roughly the same as asking, can love exist within extreme market capitalism and our extreme socialism and corporate regulation in our own Western democracy?

As a first step in what may be a very wild ride, we have to put such a question into context. We also have to define what "rumination" means in contrast to Western democracies. First, let's look at the context.

This context relates directly to what is happening within our country at this time. What we have in this country is a symptom of Western democracy, or what we may also call a government and its people pushed into extreme corners of political thought and ideas without the exigent need for rational compromise, moderation, or centrism.

There are those who are already at this centrist or moderate point as well and also those who are similarly crushed by their elegance to a peaceful and more sustainable democracy in which a greater number of citizens does well and greater numbers lead fruitful and happy lives as a collective and cooperative society. As it notes in the American Constitution, there needs to exist the pursuit of this idea of happiness. What is not guaranteed is happiness itself. Rather, one must deal with the process of getting to that point of optimal happiness without the guarantee of the deliverance of any happiness whatsoever. Therefore, we must admit that the pursuit of happiness means that the methods we need in order to arrive at an endpoint of happiness, whether that endpoint is abstract or more specific, will differ widely, as everyone within our American democracy at this time has differing and divergent ideas of what this happiness is as well as what their preferences will be once they arrive at this endpoint of happiness. And because these preferences will be wide-ranging and different, then the means and methods we use to pursue individual and group happiness must also differ widely. Some may argue that they may differ to an infinite extent and that such happiness would be impossible to quantify or even remotely describe. But before we advance any further with the idea of happiness, let's discuss the primary symptom of our democracy at this time, which is a divided government and a divided population within a two party, conflicted duopoly.

As far as American democracy is concerned, we live in a nation that may someday learn of the reasons for our current crisis. The first of these crises is the difference between zero-sum and, its opposite, cooperation and bi-partisanship plurality among two distinct entities, or in our case, our two, dominant political parties. This is the same difference between binarism, where it is either one or the other, and the other idea is what many would call pluralism, where we can both come out as winners. Currently, it seems as though that there is either one or the other, who will win in the society we are in now when playing games such as this.

This important idea of socialism, based upon European models of socialism, is guided by the general philosophy that everyone should be able to pursue their version of happiness in a more cooperative manner that generates a more limited but rational form of happiness that benefits all equally, as each one of us, as a mass of citizens, must benefit and be able to pursue a common and collective group version of happiness as documented in many historical American texts as well as in our own unique Constitution.

While there has never been a guarantee of happiness to any extent, as no one can actually know what makes all people happy at all times, then we must assert that having all people limitedly happy requires the socialist's need for a rigid equality as opposed to an unfettered, individualistic freedom. Since we live within a country that is currently suffering from binarism, we are at a unique polarized point where unfettered freedom is needed *and* the strict equality of socialism is also needed.

Very skilled theorists and public policy analysts had once accomplished such a problem several years ago. They came up with a plan to maintain both capitalism and socialism at the same time, thereby guaranteeing, what Mill would call, "the greatest good for the greatest number." But with anything that exists and yet rejects the permanence of stagnation and stalled change, such as a general collective or a collection of fierce individuals who must cooperate to realize greater benefits, no matter if one is an ardent capitalist or a desperate socialist, such a divided nation must fail when our binary system must again operate against the backdrop of any moderation or centrism that unites and fortifies any strong democracy.

For example, this unique combination of capitalism and socialism did trigger much criticism as far as theoretical grievances were concerned from all sides. Luckily, though, the collective was still able to gain a general level of happiness, while those on the more individualistic side were able to gain enough freedom to co-exist happily with those on the other.

The three branches of government, while appealing to those who wanted to exist in both ideological spheres, had still been able to co-exist with one another. It was acknowledged by the general whole that it wasn't at all perfect capitalism or a perfect socialism, but such a co-existence at least achieved acceptable levels of both at a time in the country's history when many eyed the broad horizon of a cleavage if most people were not allowed to vent their criticism of or preserve their cherished ideals in both systems of government and economy. But never was there ever a cause for alarm like the one we have now. Freedom and Equality had finally found a home within these same borders, and the prior mood swings that haunted the country in previous decades had eased into a general agreement just a couple of decades ago. We had at least arrived at a compromise that gave each citizen a certain level of equal happiness within the binary constructs that governed over us. Happiness had finally found a home within the borders of our nation. And so did freedom. And people were free to criticize and debate the merits and drawbacks of both.

Naturally, information outside of our unusually insular borders had to be controlled, but at least it kept everyone within some acceptable limit of happiness, even though at varying individual levels. Regardless of the actual numbers that may have been both positive and negative in terms of how much happiness a person had, it was at least enough to get to a point where people could tolerate a general, weakened happiness that held together freedom and equality from rending the nation apart and spiraling out of control.

Naturally, at first, most of us expected that one side would triumph over the other - that capitalism would trounce socialism, that the rich would triumph over the poor, and even though there may have been a slight bias in terms of capitalism anyway, it was only in terms of the values of the qualities of happiness that differed, as the numbers, such as the integers that could, at least theoretically, quantify happiness, for example, are different, but basically, they equaled the same as the collective happiness that equaled similar levels of happiness as a free and equal people.

Certainly, there was still the usual conflict of ideas due to our freedoms and rights, but this was buffered by the introduction of faith and not lapses of government.

Many people, other than those who relied on government, were at least cognizant that government could not be all things to all people and that faith had to work for the dissatisfied instead of the distribution of wealth through government. This held together well because, by this unique co-existence between moral faith and the continuation of the practical distribution of wealth by government, these two sides almost miraculously held together, even during the most extreme bouts with entering another war with Iraq and within the large umbrella of our collective happiness, albeit by a slim margin. And while most registered similar values of happiness, the ideological struggles that afterwards ensued, mostly due to new methods of mass information distribution among the populace, these struggles demanded the rise and the opening up of the critical question of whether or not both capitalism and socialism could really exist at the same time and within the same space.

What happened, with the flood of new information and also the new disinformation lurched upon us by new technologies, the valiant attempt to co-exist soon pushed us to opposite ends, where capitalism grew more extreme and socialism grew more extreme, thereby destroying collective happiness, while still leaving individual happiness within the hands of those few who were able to bear the costs of remaining happy. But nothing can last forever, because otherwise it would have resulted in crippling stagnation and never-ending internal conflict - perhaps internal warfare.

At this time, our society is, once again, pushed towards extreme ideologies that orbit these ideas of raw capitalism and raw socialism. These ideas have now become part of the economic and political duopoly that dubiously inhabit the same space. Also, these two ideologies are pulling us apart, as though a fissure has occurred that is both unnatural and has never before been witnessed in this country since the early 1800's and the early 1960s. And because of our binary means of deciding what our collective priorities must be, it's either the classic model of liberalism, or corporate hegemony that can win, or the classic model of socialism, or state regulation of capital industries and the protection of collective bargaining, that can win. This may be a problem with the basic concept of zero-sum or binary outcomes.

Only one candidate can win, for example. Only one trade in the stock market can win is another basic example. Even a far more distant example of this may also be in our own our computer systems. The basic computer language is made up of binary codes - 'on' or 'off' - as this is the language of numbers. Unfortunately, there is nothing to get around this binarism, whether we like it or not. Only in times of national crisis can we reach for the irrational, which is something akin to compromise, and not necessarily the trading or bargaining for greater advantage, which is just another example of needing to win or inherent binarism in this very serious and dangerous game.

To take one example, especially as it relates to this need to win and especially as it relates to winner-take-all elections, let's say we have a Republican who adamantly agrees with Democrats that legislation must be passed to address climate change. How is this same Republican supposed to vote Republican, when he or she also agrees for the need to preserve his gun rights? Similarly, how are progressive liberals supposed to support the fundamental need for gun control, when Republican legislation to give tax vouchers to those parents who want their children to attend better schools in districts other than the failing ones in their own neighborhoods would be better for them? Both Republican and Democrat have no choice but to prioritize his or her preferences when both preferences are equally important at the same time. In such a system of selecting which preferences are most important, the government is unable to represent the full range of preferences for its voters, thereby limiting the citizenry's power and their right to choose as citizens. This affords them even more power and privilege over the same people they represent.

Let's also take our current battle between our President, Donald Trump, and the current Speaker of the House, Nancy Pelosi, as another example. President Trump stands resolute in not reopening the government to pass a budget without sufficient funds for a wall or barrier that stretches across the Mexican-US border. On principle, Nancy Pelosi and her fellow Democrats reject this idea of a wall and aim, ideally, to have a more peaceful and open nation but also for a more inclusive nation that tames the need for this political football known as a border wall.

Interestingly enough, many in Congress wouldn't call Pelosi's ideal at all but a mainstream American value, as the extreme left is now of the firm belief that many of their ancestors were also immigrants, and others yearning to enter such a country as this must also have the same opportunities as their own ancestors. Hence, we have a widening gap among two distinct ideas circling the same singular issue. But these ideas have coalesced into a fertile battle over fundamental principles as well as practical considerations. This can be trouble, especially when there may be other, strategic needs either to block these illegal immigrants' entry or to permit it.

As a wise Victor Hugo once wrote, "a Prince is nothing beside a Principle." The border wall is essential if the President plans to continue his presidency past his single term. And if the Speaker of The House caves in to the President, they risk losing a battle that they could have normally won and also risk the capture of the Presidency in the next election, which takes place in 2020. Meanwhile, as of now, the government remains shut down, with roughly 800,000 federal employees forced into labor without pay until the shutdown ends. Consequently, these families are suddenly suffering, especially those with children to feed and families to support.

There are those, of course, who are not suffering at all, but according to recent news reports from almost every major news outlet in the country, both flagrantly politically conservative and flagrantly politically liberal in their biases, the country is now rife with suffering as a result of this shutdown. This includes the cities and towns all across this nation that depend on local government workers to support their businesses. In other words, because there is little will to compromise, and because the two polarized parties have nothing or little to gain from compromise, the government remains closed, the federal workers are forced into labor without the exchange of their labors for their usual inelastic goods and services, and a dangerous pall of suffering overshadows our prosperous democracy.

At this point, it is very hard to say if anyone will budge for the good of the country, because there is very little, politically, to gain from compromise or even the capacity to bargain for this higher good.

Such is our situation, and such is the pressing need for this incredibly mysterious idea called "love" - the responsible ability to compromise, not to win, but perhaps, even to act irrationally instead of either winning or losing, thereby scuttling our binary approach. It is the abandonment of self-interest to win a zero-sum game and instill compromise for the good of the country and also its survival. As Anthony Downs concluded so long ago, there is really no reason to vote at all, since there is no economically realized gain. Similarly, the only reason why people vote is because there exists some irrational need to be socially responsible that has nothing to do with self-interest. Even though any concept of "love" is really unknowable, it just may be the only trick we have in solving this perplexing riddle of our current political crisis, especially as the next Presidential election swiftly approaches.

Again, there is nothing to gain by compromise by government. And yet, as predicted by many before, a looming American conflict does loom larger in the distant horizon, or at least this is a fear by many who observe this phenomenon. The thought of such a conflict can be horrifying, depending on how one measures the severity of the crisis, but it is no longer such a joke, as some have thought. For some reason, since there is little to gain by compromising on institutionalized principles in a zero-sum battle, the only real way to solve such a dilemma is by utilizing the irrational as an effective strategy and incentive for compromise. This is what we mean by "love" within this context - the need for political altruism and sacrifice with very little to gain individually, but a sacrifice through compromise that keeps our nation intact. This is for the general welfare of the multiplying numbers of those who are suffering and to save our country from the essential conflict that arises over conflicting principles and conflicting, polarized ideologies.

There are many ways in which we may approach the complexity of this idea of "love," which remains so mysterious and irrational, within a general discussion of both extreme socialist and extreme capitalist paradigms. We are not talking about magical thinking, though, when it comes to "love" within this current context. With the wealth of information that is now available to us, mostly due to advancements in technology, it may be permissible to jump from a variety different disciplines to come to the ultimate conclusion that this idea of "love" can exist within both extreme spheres of political thought and also within the same space. Many would object to this, because many would think it extremely important to maintain one's focus on one's specific line of thought and political belief and work from there to a zero-sum outcome.

For example, at least in the realm of academia, an English professor would never permit a discussion of William Golding's *Lord of the Flies* to co-exist in a classroom with the political theories and philosophies of Locke and Hobbes. Similarly, a political science professor would never permit a biological or even a psychological discussion of the Original Position or Social Contract outside of the narrow realm of political science. And yet if we find ourselves zeroing in on one particular discipline, we may lose the opportunity to have a discussion on political science and mathematics, or English and cultural theory, for example. Therefore, it is important to fuse or combine disciplines within the same space to develop a more practical, feasible, and dare we say, more reliable method of ending this widening chasm between two extremes of ideology. There at least has to be a general movement towards a happy middle-ground, where all are happy but somewhat miserable *simultaneously*. But how can we be both happy and sad simultaneously?

This is where the mystery of "Love" comes into play. From what little we may understand of such a concept, "love" can also be rational and irrational, sublime and subterranean, euphoric and downright depressing, all at the same time. Of course, the definition of "love" cannot be pinned down to such basic terms, which is why the term "love" is in quotation marks. Whether or not "love" can be defined or even safely contemplated is not the general point here. The point is that "love" will always be a factor in all disciplines and in all of the tenets of socialism and capitalism whether we would like to admit it or not. Also, for the purposes of this discussion, it is important to take "love" out of its quotation marks and at least make the somewhat plausible assumption that love does exist within both economic and political paradigms of socialism and capitalism, even though, under certain assumptions and interpretations of this concept of love, love may not fit in this way at all. The question now becomes, how can we find love anywhere within the context of extreme socialism, one hand, and extreme capitalism on the other within a functioning democracy?

Since we can assume that love can be both irrational and rational at the same time, we can be safe in assuming that there is such a concept as love, and there are only a few ways we are able to define it in terms of a larger, more political discussion of where love may or may not fit between these two extremes of political thought. In other words, we may be too adventurous in our pursuit to heighten or even discount love's importance within both paradigms, but if we can at least admit that love can be both rational and irrational at the same time, then we can label such an investigation and examination of love as both pleasurable as well as painful, especially when a concept so mysterious as love is applied to even the most rudimentary principles of socialism and capitalism. But if the concept of love does contain parts of the irrational, then how can we even think about moving forward when we do not have a definition of love that can be definitively rational, especially as far as any political discussion goes? Where can we start this examination amid the backdrop of the more concrete political theories of extreme socialism and extreme capitalism?

To say that such a discussion can exist in the first place is not necessarily an apology for the following discussion and all of its glaring mistakes and weaknesses. Rather, love can exist if we can at least place it within a historical context about prior ideas of love, no matter how far-fetched such a concept is.

For example, the philosopher Plato delineated this almost-impossible and incredibly difficult concept of love, and even though his delineation belongs to ancient history and is perhaps too historical and ancient to take seriously, there did exist another man who built on Plato's ideas and applied it at a time when there may have been no concrete or specific evidence at all for love's existence and operation with any political paradigm. This historical figure is Dr. Martin Luther King, Jr.

As Plato contemplated love, so did King apply Plato's delineation to political thought and practice. You can even go so far as to define Dr. King as a political philosopher as well as a practical activist. As with Plato, King brought his concept of love to the forefront of a wider political theory, and dare we say, a very practical political theory at that. Plato would have been very impressed.

This is why we can at least structure this examination in terms of *Eros, Philia, and Agape* - the essential, albeit ancient examples of love's mysterious operation, whether the existence of love can be proven, quantified, or qualified. Again, the assumption is that traces of love can exist within both extremes of socialism and capitalism, and if we can envision a love that can exist within both extremes, we can also argue that the fissure of both ideologies within the same occupied space can be reunified, thereby preventing a conflict that threatens to separate our country into two separate entities.

Yet in the absence of a purely rational theory, how do we even begin to apply this ancient concept of love in terms of both socialism and capitalism? This can only be possible if we are able to jump from one discipline to the another and fuse disciplines together and form, not necessarily an airtight theory but at the very least, to understand love's operation within two extreme and volatile camps, given our political situation at this time. This can be best accomplished and discussed through a process known as "rumination."

Interestingly enough, rumination is best described by many contemporary psychologists as an illness and not an association of thoughts that should be replicated, employed, applied, or carried out. In many ways, these intrepid psychologists are right in their suspicions of rumination, especially here in the Western world. The point is not to argue or belabor the point whether or not rumination is or is not an illness, but it is the current position of many accomplished psychologists at this time that rumination is a deep and depressing brooding. And brooding can lead to disastrous results if one uses it too much without licensed assistance or proper guidance. But rumination, when it comes to this overall discussion, can still be useful if we can at least remain focused on the bigger picture of arresting the conflicts and paradoxes of political thought that the nation faces at this very moment. We can use such a rumination in the combination and amalgamation of other, separate disciplines to establish a general whole that may end the extremism on both sides of the political divide.

Of course, rumination is dangerous psychologically, but in terms of the application of love's mystery to a general argument for the existence of love, rumination, especially given the breadth of the digital information now available, does serve a valuable function. Through rumination, we can at least take that one small step in a journey that may indeed end in terrible failure and illness. But we don't really know if it will fail or end in illness at all, since there is no solid empirical evidence yet of such an illness ending that way.

We can say that this book is more of a rumination of love more than anything else, because such an application to extreme capitalism and socialism demands that we ruminate on these ideas just to get the ball rolling in that general direction in order use a multiplicity of viewpoints and disciplines to bridge our widening partisan gap. In other words, as Chinese philosophy reminds us, this is but one childlike step in a journey of a thousand miles, and rumination is at the beginning of this wandering and nomadic journey.

Also, we can say this work is nothing more than a simple rumination. This doesn't pretend to be a penetrating political theory or any sort of politically scientific cure for our current national crisis. Instead, since the nation is now amid the partisan extremes of political thinking, and now that most of the citizens here are concerned over this huge gulf among the two opposing parties, there really is no alternative but to ruminate and find a solution to this great divide that threatens us. Actually, this book may not help with the healing and unity of the nation at all. What it can do, however, is find the least bit of love in both political systems, and should that love exist in both, it is highly possible, then, that this application of love to the militant separation of ideas and two opposing streams of ideas that continues to haunt our current politics can make a difference bringing wholeness and completeness to our conflicted democracy.

We are also finally beginning to understand as well that we don't necessarily have to be an exceptional country in order to be a truly happy one. But first we have to accept rumination here as an ally and not so much as a sickness. Those who remain fiercely disciplined in their approach to questions of politics may find this book useless, if not downright uncouth and mildly insulting. And while this may be so, the application of love to both drifting sides of our political principles and conventional political practices will at least make some advancement towards the initiation of further study. Let's hope this rumination is able to do just that.

Eros

If Greek *Eros* is defined by aesthetic beauty and romantic love, then there must be an examination of whether *Eros* can be found in both systems of government. The first exploration of this should begin with capitalism. Socialism will be discussed a little later.

Currently, the economy here in the United States is doing well. There are some fears of recession, but other than that, most are benefiting from an economy of scale, mainly because with more currency flooding the marketplace, people are able to trade their labors for more costly and moral goods, such as airline travel, gifts, and even getting married, depending on where an our informed citizenry falls on the capitalist or socialist divide.

Eros can take place in capitalism, but there are limits indeed. Those who own the means of production will benefit the most, as very low corporate tax rates and fierce competition among corporate monopolies continue to trade and, thereby, provide goods and services to a populace that may not be able to afford them. Here, it is important to note that capitalism, which is an economic theory most of all, demands that taxes are low, and this may result in negative externalities that are not are completely ignored by national and more localized governments that decide to uphold capitalism within the economy or at least fight towards that end. In other words, the wealthy benefit from extreme capitalism and will fight for it, and the theory now becomes that this wealth will trickle down to the extreme socialists who support helping the poor, the most vulnerable, and especially, those who must trade their strenuous and more arduous labors to achieve even the most meager of goods and services.

In such an environment, the socialists get it last, while most of the wealth remains with the raw capitalists at the top. Yet the children of wealth are often labeled as 'trust fund babies' and the like for taking part in their parent's hard work, luck, and fortune. Elements of wealth from parents that are given to their children, like trust funds, are often bemoaned by the poor, lower middle classes, and even central middle classes, even though many of these financial vehicles are taxed whenever income is withdrawn from them.

Inheritance and the freedom to pass down wealth to children will always be a problem in Western societies. Inheritance will always perpetuate the great divide between rich and poor. Add to this the problem of wealthy mating habits among other wealthy families and the privileged connections these yields and that compounds the problem.

Yet there is no telling if the children of the wealthy will play their cards right to maintain such wealth, or that their values and spending habits their wealthy parents have instilled within them will ensure their financial wellbeing and level of power. Some parents make their children earn their money before passing it on to them after death, while other parents opt to give their children everything they've ever dreamt of that they themselves were denied when they were young.

In a socialist society within a democracy, many argue that the economy, guaranteed by subsidies and close corporate regulation, would increase spending, not from the top down, but from the bottom up. This would especially help poor communities that hope to take a more equitable part in participating in a more business-oriented system, not to mention the more obvious benefit of aiding the poor and the sick. What's more, the aspirations of the bourgeois would no longer rely solely on the very rich. They would also have to rely on the subsidized poor and the central middle classes that have traditionally relied on the bourgeoisie for much-needed capital. By the bottom-up approach, socialism can make the same difference as anything remotely trickle-down. It's simply a question of priorities.

The push upwards in spending does bolster the lower and middle classes but not necessarily the bourgeois. The wealthy do not benefit at all, as they are taxed at a much higher rate to benefit social ills and other societal problems that are, arguably, not of their own making, such as poverty, sickness, and the lack of health care among the poor. They must also subsidize the disabled and unemployable through Social Security and Medicare. The wealthy have to be taxed, though, because charity never works as well as higher taxes.

But as it relates directly to trickle-down economics, which has been the cornerstone of American economic policy for several generations of conservative economic policy now, corporations, then, are able to function more freely, and therefore, there soon becomes the problem of inflation that has to be checked often to make sure those who benefit can afford the same quality of goods as those who do not receive the same benefits. The main difference among goods, then, is the quality of goods. It is not hard to imagine, though, that only the owners of the means of production will actually achieve a greater form of happiness, while the poor must wait until the wealth trickles down to them. This effect is bound to happen sooner or later, and for those staunch supporters of socialism, it doesn't happen at all. Therefore, capitalism must be buffered through some sort of regulation in order to avoid conflict. Whatever regulations that are put in place, such as a rise of minimum wage to all workers within national and state boundaries, must be fought for and voted on, if the will to vote and fight exists.

But at the federal level, capitalist theory would mandate cutting budgets to allow capitalism in its free form to thrive, even during times of intense public outcries for the health and preservation of the least well-off. Moral public goods and services that are normally provided through government taxes are also slashed to make room for more privatized goods that socialists will have to buy despite the need to bring individuals into socialism's much sought-after condition of universal equality. So, we can define capitalism at this time as forging corporate happiness but only for those who can pay enough to be owners of production. Those who are not owners but laborers instead and those who may also one day own the means of production, should they continue to trade their labors for cheaper corporate goods, may also survive, provided they themselves become the owners of production only if they pursue ownership. So if the poor pursue ownership, there is opportunity.

A family purchasing a small business, for example, may be suppressed and eliminated by eager corporate bodies but may still compete with corporations that have far more leverage in terms of purchasing power. Yes, corporations are often too large and slow to adapt to changing conditions as small business as often can, but no matter what direction these small businesses take, they will never match the sheer power of a corporation looking to buy some of these successful smaller businesses on the cheap or simply provide goods and services that are more widely available, in terms of the information a population receives, that also fall under a corporation's control and domination.

If raw capitalism in this instance does take place, then there must also be a more defined class hierarchy that comes along with it as an externality of corporate wealth. The division of classes is more rigidly defined, because those who possess more wealth and more capital will benefit from the continued stream of low-cost labor that is traded very cheaply. It is safe to say, then, that the idea of *Eros* will cost the wealthy much less than those who demand that more cooperation and more regulation to realize *Eros* within their own lives as socialists must compromise.

Even in times of extreme and raw capitalism, or even in cases of political libertarianism, *Eros* is still available, but only for those few who are most wealthy, and, therefore, have a better chance of achieving a greater happiness. This, however, is by no means an unbending rule that oppresses the least well-off of us either. *Eros*, or at least it's slow beginnings, can exist within a rigid class system that only benefits the few, but it is rare that the least well-off of us will glean as much happiness from it. There just may be the inability to express *Eros* within poor families, especially sick families that are too jaded by their inability to grow financially in a system that benefits only those with enough purchasing power.

For example, a wealthy family may encourage their young daughter to pursue her dream of being a famous painter, while another daughter of a poor or sick family does not have the same chances of success at being a painter that the wealthy daughter has. Naturally, the poor and the sick family may encourage a daughter's artistry as a sideline hobby, but the further we move down to the least well-off family, the more likely it will be that a young daughter will move towards more vocational goals than continue her artistry or preserve her natural talents. The poor and sick daughter must give up her talents and apply herself to harder labor so that she can earn a living, even though she may not be talented in the labor she is forced into.

We can safely say, then, that raw capitalism, as we have now, while at least regulated by a few states rather than a centralized federal government, can in no way bring *Eros* to everyone. Rather, just like any system in its most extreme form, it can only be upheld and benefit those at the top rather than those on the bottom and focuses the goal of ownership on the poorest among us. This may be an obvious point, but the important point of this is not so obvious.

Eros, being different for all classes, can also exist for the least well-off, because *Eros* can change shape and form and present itself in different ways as we move down the strict social class ladder. So due to *Eros* operating within both wealthy as well as with poor and sick families, there must also be a link that unifies both the wealthy and the poor and sick. In other words, even though extremely capitalistic societies do share *Eros* in common, and because there is a benefit for those who need *Eros* in their lives, there is at least more of an interest in preserving it and cooperating to ensure its existence.

Certainly, there can be very little social mobility when unregulated capitalism operates, but to assume that *Eros* operates only with the wealthy at the top is a belief that is too specious to take seriously. *Eros* can thrive even within very poor or very sick or very dysfunctional groups, as stated, because at least there is more freedom, perhaps, to pursue *Eros* on one's own cooperative terms regardless of the disparities in income and class.

For instance, *Eros* may exist for those on the highest rungs of the class ladder, only because more wealth exists, but it is also safe to say that wealth itself doesn't necessarily lead to greater happiness or success either, especially among those who are born privileged or those who have immediate success, because corporations continue to remain unregulated. Moreover, the wealthy few do not necessarily have the same freedoms to pursue *Eros* as those who are the least well-off.

What binds intimate couples together, for instance, may be a dream of one day buying a yacht to sail around the world. This may mean more success in monetary terms and material goods, but the plain fact that a wealthy couple needs a yacht to ensure *Eros'* active operation and evolution within their romantic lives is not necessarily a measure of *Eros* that leads to a greater and sustainable happiness.

To a poor family, it may be that the freedom to make love without any direct or indirect barriers to making love creates a sense of *Eros* that is more harmonious and less acrimonious in terms of the mysteries of realized and practical *Eros*. In short, the old adage remains. Money can't buy us love. Surely, it helps with all other aspects of our happiness and prosperity, but money will never be able to ensure *Eros'* existence in the lives of the social elite. Actually, much empirical evidence suggests the opposite.

Instead, most of us understand that *Eros* exists in many shapes, shades, and forms. These shapes, shades, and forms may change over time and among the various levels of the class structure. For example, for a young couple just starting out in the world, *Eros* may lead them into a life-long relationship, but just when *Eros* seems to be absent, it strengthens its hold on this financially strained couple. A new child by this same least well-off couple becomes the product of a blossoming *Eros* that starts anew from the essential act of reproduction. So then it turns out that the least well-off in our extreme capitalistic paradigm can also realize *Eros*. Without *Eros'* procession and widespread distribution to even the most least-well off of us, we may be in big trouble.

It may start by making romantic love. And perhaps it starts anew by creating families that bond wayward strangers more closely, and eventually, leads to more complex or even ethereal and celestial, forms of love. Raw capitalism, then, in terms of the benefits that are given, may benefit the wealthy in terms of dollars, but not necessarily in terms of romantic love. It is safe to say, then, that the least well-off may also realize this evolution of *Eros*, if they are ever able to migrate socially to higher levels through the love they instill within their own children. This is but one example. *Eros* may also occur through romantic love among the least well-off and does not necessarily require procreation.

And yet within even the most rigid social order, love has the ability to exist, shift into such mysterious forms such that the least well-off can achieve parity with wealthy families.

This link seems to make logical sense here, even though *Eros* is something completely irrational and goes beyond the assumptions made in public choice preferences. Usually more often than not, the major public choice assumption is self-interest, and with *Eros* the assumption is that both self-interest and the collectively interested can experience *Eros* at the same time, although within totally different classes and totally conflicting political camps.

The more we approach an equilibrium, whether politically or economically, the greater the likelihood that such a sought-after stability can make *Eros* more available to the whole of the nation, and therefore, an equilibrium, when it arrives, can show us that even the extremities of political thought can remain in place and exist, while those within the bloated middle may also be showered with such a grace that reaches into yet another form of *Eros*. Having equilibrium for any society ought to be the envy of the world.

Such extremes in ideologies or even the extremism in the theories that fight for a niche in the wider political spectrum we have available to us is not an optimal condition for *Eros* to operate. Of course, we are making the assumption that *Eros* benefits the most when there are fewer political extremes in existence. But at least we may also say that there is at least a connection within raw capitalism and tethered capitalism that foils the ruthless war of ideas among capitalists and socialists that currently progresses towards an inevitably tragic end.

The connection that *Eros* forges between raw capitalism in a more practical world that benefits only the few, however, and a kinder capitalism that benefits even greater numbers suggests that there can be a compromise between those who support rugged individualism and those who veer a little towards the middle with a softer, more compassionate form of capitalism. The middle, or the political center, is probably the best place to ensure this compromise. Should that center lack traction, however, we must then assume that raw capitalism and extreme socialism cannot exist within the same space, even though there can be at least the opportunity and desire by many moderates and centrists to share the same space. If this is the case, then we no longer have any collective at all, but a society that is at war with itself, and therefore, a society that must break in two and exist as separate, distinct entities, simply because it is pulled apart by the extremes.

Neither could happiness exist, until yet another equilibrium is established within both separate spheres - one purely capitalist, the other purely socialist. In sum, there would exist the pressing need for some upheaval, usually a violent and destructive one, to establish yet another equilibrium where the two are separated. This upheaval not only neutralizes *Eros* but ensures that there can be no happiness to pursue for both separate spheres. The two spheres now become mutually exclusive. "Together we stand. Divided we fall."

For *Eros* to return, it would take a very long time, while each space finds some artificial form of stability in *Eros'* absence. Even when both spheres break into their own separate selves, our public will be motivated more by fear of the other than by any other possible motivation. *Eros* can bridge that gap, but only within the proper rhythm and cadence that an equilibrium can bring within the same space. A stable equilibrium can only be formed through the virtue of patience and the healing effects of time. So, we can at least assume here that two separate spheres are still able to reunite, given *Eros'* common existence between them. Extreme capitalism and extreme socialism, then, share *Eros* in common within our democracy.

The same can be said of a socialist economy and government. A new equilibrium would have to be reached, but there will always remain a link in terms of *Eros* between extreme socialism and any form of raw capitalism. But *Eros* is experienced differently, because in socialism instead of the more individualistic strength to maintain or augment one's own personal wealth, within socialist societies the currency is mainly power among a collection of individuals. A socialist environment attempts to find a happy equilibrium where equality is shared but power is not shared. Nevertheless, there are still the benefits of *Eros* in extreme socialism, and once again, just to drive the point home, *Eros* exists even in the politics of extreme socialist democracies as well.

In extreme socialism, what we have is the state regulation of corporations and industry, higher taxes on wealth and income, and greater benefits for the working poor, the sick, the impoverished, and the disenfranchised. The balance of happiness realized by our citizens is favored in terms of the lower classes rather than the wealthy elite as well as the bourgeoisie, and perhaps even an eroding middle class, but what is achieved instead is a balance that can best be described as fair and equally applied, regardless of income or purchasing power. Yet as a result of this higher equality, there must remain a power structure that remains in place that makes decisions on how best to repair, manage, and govern the populace.

Granted that everyone within such a system is more unified in terms of equal wealth, but by the sheer force of our Constitution and our electoral governance within a democratic system, there must still be a democratically elected government, and there still needs to be adequate representation for the range of political beliefs. So even though individual wealth will be more in line with everyone's general collective wealth, there will still be the externalities and conflicts of who governs, who decides, and who achieves the most representation within a democratic society when capitalism begins to fade into the annals of short-term history and more socialist laws and policies take shape. In other words, while people may be joined by the happiness of parity of wealth and purchasing power, there still must remain the binarism of winner-take-all elections and the competition, not for dollars, but for power and for recognition.

This may seem disconcerting, but actually *Eros* is still found within both extremes, because both systems, as older operations fade into history, must at least have commonalities and certain new freedoms that are shared in common. In other words, the dollars and benefits may change hands, and the powerful may jockey for greater positions of political control and importance, but this time, the cultural changes are sweeping, and as a result of this more cultural change, there is both adaptation among the wealthy and greater happiness among the least-well off. In other words, *Eros* is also available even to the most steadfast and ardent capitalists in a democratic economy.

Let's take sex and sin as an example and the functions of *Eros* operating within, not the economics or politics of extreme socialism, but within the *culture* of extreme socialism. Since morality within a culture is handled more by religious sects and groups, sex and sin, instead, are managed by the state. Through historical patterns, we can find that the state, within democratic extreme socialism, will legislate to regulate, not the morality or sexual behaviors of a populace, but the safety of a populace during permitted and decriminalized sexual behaviors that had once been considered sins. Issues like guaranteeing a woman's right to govern her own body by safe birth control and emergency contraception on the one hand, and cost-efficient abortions and the normalization of adoption on the other will abrogate the culture of sex extend the limits of sin. Also, safe sex using condoms and effective birth control in a more sexually liberated culture, where the culture of sex and sin will be more collectively orchestrated and more evenly distributed, can benefit even the most extreme defenders of capitalism who no longer have access to excessive forms of sex and sin. Similarly, the prohibition of alcohol and drugs will be relaxed, such that the focus again will be on the safety and pleasure of the collective and less on the reliance of the individual and his or her own responsibilities for his or her sexual and leisurely life.

Just as Lenin had predicted for communist societies, having sex will be as simple and free as having a glass of water. Of course, our important religious institutions will be adversely affected, as the government will now legislate where the church can no longer impose its doctrines, but there is more collective freedom, since class structures are narrowed to include even the wealthiest, holiest, and especially, the poorest among us. Therefore, *Eros* can operate here, in terms of sex and sin, at least, to narrow cultural divides, as each individual remains more securely protected, not through abstinence per se, but through the free availability of sex and sin that is the result of a dramatic but beneficial shift in culture. It is now feasible to imagine that a wealthy American industrialist or the imperial capitalist can now have a passionate romance with a young struggling college student with very few repercussions and fewer consequences in terms of the shifting cultural norms that socialism brings. This, again, may be obvious, but the real point here is that no longer does sex and sin belong only to those with great wealth. Granted that once stable and unified families will tend to break apart, but there is no longer the threat to the wealthy of pursuing relationships that they would like to explore with other men or women that had once been shunned and at times prohibited.

The new culture of sexual and social liberation, this new extreme socialist system within a democracy, will permit sex and sin to much greater degrees, and all the while the priority becomes greater safety and less governance by the moral teachings of synagogues, mosques, temples, and churches.

The same goes for those who identify with the LBGTQ community. Because religion plays a lesser role in democratic extreme socialism, there is much more freedom for these battered and unique communities to thrive. Also, all religions, regardless of their numbers of followers or their multiplicity and diversities of doctrine will separate from the state and compete for members to a much lesser degree. Racial tensions will also be eased. The struggle for happiness now aims, not for wealth, but for political power and control.

Black-Americans, for example, will have the chance to demonstrate how prosperous they have been by their engagement on the political fault lines of American society, assuming that the majority of Black-Americans are more to the left than right. These Black-Americans may not have adequate wealth or enough representation in extreme capitalist societies, but in terms of sheer power, political skill, and the greater awareness that recognition brings, they have the opportunity to shine during a period of economic parity, political equality, and greater social justice.

While all of this is already known, we must also make the important point that within this new socialist society, *Eros* changes again to suit a swing in the opposite direction.

Romance can also be found despite narrower class differences. And so the culture itself is again transformed by valuable individual preferences when the opposite reaction to extreme capitalism occurs. The relativity, if not the outright preservation of sex and sin will again morph to serve the interests and protection of the wealthy and the benefits among the upper classes, but the greater breadth of *cultural Eros* will be made available to the lower classes in the socialist extreme. In fact, the more extreme the socialism when capitalism makes a return, the greater possibility and opportunity for *Eros*, if only socialists can prevent morality in legislation. In terms of sex and sin, more freedoms will flourish but not the importance of uniform equality. This will create, at the very least, an illusion of stagnation in terms of wealth, but will advance *Eros* by benefiting the collective whole and not just the elite few.

Extreme Democratic Socialism and extreme Democratic Capitalism make this possible, as the common thread is not only *Eros*, but also our democracy as a more proportionally representative system. It is apparent that *Eros*, in all its myriad and evolving forms, can even exist in non-democratic societies as well, as brutal as some of them may seem on the surface of our own government's misinformation, disinformation, and propaganda.

But it is very important to note here that this new extremely socialistic culture that will find equilibrium at some point, will be buffered, not by the state itself, but by the individuals and their growing sense of the need for individualistic freedom within that collective state. Individuals within a more democratic state, however, will now still compete for power and the power to make decisions as to where the state's priorities and collective labors should be focused. There is still inherent competition, if not the all-out struggle for power and recognition and not necessarily a rat-race for material goods and wealth. Individuals will still compete, just for different types of rewards.

This can be a sad reality for most extremely socialistic societies, however, and especially communist ones, but we can at least find some elements of capitalism within an expanding socialist environment. In extreme capitalistic societies, it is money and purchasing power that guarantees power. But under extreme socialist governance, it is more the opportunity to narrow the classes, consolidate labor, and prioritize such inelastic goods and services, as health care and the opportunity of greater love, in all its forms, to operate among the whole collective. This has never been realized just yet by robust economies and also the legislation that fall beyond the realms of democratic societies.

Luckily, our society remains a democracy where both systems may still exist simultaneously through the fluidity and evolution of *Eros* as a cultural and well-earned element, a common thread, link, or connection between two extremes that are very similar in terms of their opportunity to experience *Eros*, just in different ways.

Yet the struggle becomes a scramble for greater power and control, and this is a dangerous bi-product, or externality, of the socialist state. With capitalist economies, the struggle is more for individual characteristics that benefit the person, like the virtue of a good and well-rounded character. In the near-opposite system, the virtue of character matters less. More citizens, however, are at liberty to narrow barriers when these barriers are attenuated by the policies and the legislation of the state. This can happen so long as a nation can realize *Eros* along with relatively equal *quantities* of goods, and for capitalistic societies the greater availability and opportunities to capture a greater *quality* of goods and services, even for the least-well off.

If there are power struggles in a socialistic society, however, through any sort of violence, protest, military intervention, or general strike, however, these are more likely a result of the lack of economic freedoms and opportunities that a parity of wages and a shortage of morality bring among the populace. Such struggles for liberation and power in extreme socialist societies usually involve a struggle for a higher quality of life, material goods, better services, and the greater and wider choices that capitalism brings. This is mainly because capitalism is more of an economic system than more of a holistic economic and political system like that of socialism.

Many ardent socialists appreciate the socialist ideal that labors are common and evenly distributed among all people, and so culture remains a bit closer to heaven on earth. Yet socialistic culture, in its extreme form, does not offer an adequate treatment for the unfairness of disposing of an individual's natural talents, when that individual may benefit more by the development of individual natural talents. These divided natural talents are neutralized by a state that normally would have assured greater equality in a fixed and corrupt capitalistic one. Whatever remnants of natural talents remain are utilized within governing bodies for the acquisition of power and not necessarily wealth or material gain, unless corruption by these individual bodies are involved. For example, many Soviets in positions of power still craved and acquired luxury Western goods, while most of their people went without them. Without doubt, like the deepening separation of the wealthy from the poor in democratic capitalism, the deepening divides of power within the state can ruin nations and instead create new dictatorships and totalitarian tyrannies where free democracies ought to have been.

To those who have the displeasure of living within a dictatorship or totalitarian society, tyranny, distributed evenly by the one or the masses, along with control and fear, is established to eliminate the risk of liberation or dissent in any form. *Eros*, then, has little chance in such conditions, even though it may exist at the very top with the dictator, the party, or functionaries and loyal advisors to both.

The military may benefit, but only in terms of the booty gained and the false and valueless conduct that comes along with rape, looting, and threats of destruction. Think of a jail where innocent people are being held hostage by the policies of a very few men and women. Add to that human rights abuses and the like.

Most democratic societies, even in their political and economic extremes, understand the human toll this tyranny takes in all areas of human life. Even though a democratic system is certainly neither perfect nor a panacea for any of its own, stubborn, and prevailing social ills, dictatorships and totalitarian regimes are far worse. Even more constitutional monarchies, where *Eros* is at least distributed from the top down, are preferred over tyrannical dictatorships and completely equal societies. While we should all know this by now, especially when we compare dictatorships to

Western Democracies, the important point here is that in dictatorships and totalitarian regimes, there is little chance for *Eros* and no connection, indirectly or directly, to the people under such tyranny.

Many would still argue that at minimum an equilibrium between a dictator and his or her subjects can be established anyway over a significant course of time. But there is no chance of *Eros* ever linking the dictator to his or her subjects, and there is scant chance that a dictatorship can establish any equilibrium or optimality at all. There is only one rule, and *Eros* is distributed only to a dictator's most loyal servants and those who are able to do this dictator's bidding.

After the illusion of *Eros* gradually spreads within a nation of growing unhappiness, discontent, and unrest, even if the dictator appears to be a saint, a father-figure, or even a matriarch to his or her subjects, there still remains the corruption and abuse of money and power that leads to a quick coup d'etat during equilibrium, instability in that underdevelopment, and a severe lack of *Eros* through a failure of politics, which we'll call warfare. Enough said on any such link of *Eros* operating at the political and economic whims of a dictator or totalitarian state, whether with fascism or communism.

A democratic society under the alternating conditions of extreme capitalism and then extreme socialism, or the optimal condition where both forms of governance can moderately co-exist at the same time, begs the question - is the link between the extreme pendular shifts of any democracy a result of a democratic constitution or the result of the now-obvious link or *Eros* between a wayward political divide that can join even the most distant and polarized political ideologies, disparities of wealth, and divisions of general happiness? Or is it democracy, as a political idea and concept, or even a practice, that links these two extremes more than *Eros* ever could?

This is really a question for the ages, because the political climate that exists now within its own context of the ever-deepening political divide between both reactionary ideologies, beliefs, and values in their extremes, if taken as two separate political spheres vying for power in an election year, is neither feasible nor reliable. This not only pertains to the operation of *Eros* to but its operation and existence of all forms of love.

In other words, we cannot have a functioning democracy. We cannot have *Eros* for all people. Stagnation is the result without the ability to find *Eros*, even though our society may remain democratic, both in theory and practice.

The link of democracy may be feasible, but the result of the missing link that *Eros* would have normally filled in our world would create certain dystopia. Similarly, a society where the only force operating is *Eros* among all can be feasible, at least if imagined or conceived, but in no way can be reliable. Interestingly enough, only a system that contains love in all three forms as discussed earlier *and* a solid footing in democracy operating as two common links and unifying, healing forces between the two extremes of socialism and capitalism are both feasible as well as reliable, even during the polarization and seemingly political separateness of an internally warring nation.

Our internal battles continue to fester as we head into an election that grows increasingly out of control. This warring alone will not necessarily threaten the operation and proper functioning of *Eros*, though. Compromises must accompany a democracy, simply because the extremes do not see a common connection at the moment, and therefore, there is no basis or benefit or even the simple motivation to war completely without *Eros* present in both paradigms. Our democracy cannot function without as *Eros* as it stands at the moment. We still have a chance if we still have *Eros* as an essential link within both extremes of a democratic society.

Philia

If we are to shed light of the effects of *Eros* within a polarized democracy and electorate, *Eros* is even more different as far as its full effects on the love family and friends share within both extremes of socialism and capitalism. This is most likely because every family has different dynamics, whether that family is extended or not. It is far easier to discuss *Eros* existing in capitalistic societies rather than extreme socialist societies, simply because the United States has mostly remained capitalistic, and historically, we have received very little research on Russian families during the Cold War, when news and ideas from the Soviet Union were squelched, despite communist sympathizers and scholars in the Western world. Because there is scant information available of how family and friends were structured and had behaved in the Soviet Union, accept perhaps by specious research and anecdotal evidence, we really don't know how *Eros* played a role in these extremely socialistic conditions. We can only speculate how these families and friends were arranged by knowing what little we learned about socialism, and its extreme, which in Soviet Union's case, was communism. In other words, families in capitalistic societies are familiar to us, while families and friendships in extreme socialistic nations are still largely an unknown, given propaganda, disinformation, and insular media coverage of the world outside of the United States. *Philia*, however, like *Eros*, links both extremes in this case as well.

The Sting song with the lyrics, "Russians love their children too," makes sense in all societies, no matter how extreme or dysfunctional any society is politically. We can attribute this to the environmental and genetic dispositions involved in relationships between parents and their children and friends. *Philia*, we can safely say, without research but with simple common sense, more often than not exists in political environments that include dictatorships and other despotic regimes. But what we can't assume about each extreme political structure is the plain fact that families, even though they usually share a basic love of each other and their friends, have to be arranged differently and must adapt to changing political and economic boundaries of differing political systems. In other words, families and friendships within both theories of extreme socialism and extreme capitalism, as well as the political realities of both, must be arranged and limited differently according to the policies and unwritten laws that govern capitalism on the one side hand and socialism on the other.

Socialism, which we will address first, and especially extreme socialism, stresses the equality of families in relation to other families. Sure, claims Tolstoy, that every family is miserable in their own unique way, but the same can be said for raw capitalistic families as well. The arrangements and patterns of economy and development within families and friendships are mostly controlled by the state, as the state mostly controls human behavior to keep families, not necessarily free, but equal. Socialism within any context will always stress equality. And because there is equality, not only among families and friends, but also among separate families occupying the same space, it follows that these families and friendships are extended in socialist societies. This is because the socialist state makes prices stable and affordable and aims to make its families equal to each other.

It logically follows that if individual parity is enforced by the state, then parents must also abide by stressing equality among their children and among their friends. In other words, unless there is a genuine fear of demographic overpopulation, like China, socialism permits families to become extended, as there is little risk to families and their friends in terms of a free market where natural talents are stressed and where an imposed, regulated environment is not stressed. Also, extreme socialist societies enforce their family policies and their ideologies of how a family should function and what friendships stick through propaganda, punishment, and excommunication. The extreme socialist political structure then becomes more totalitarian in nature, because it enforces a natural belief in equality more so than freedom, and in order to equalize and even neutralize the divisions of labor and class differences, families must follow along for the socialist state to be functional. Recognition comes from families and friends who are loyal to the state, as the freedom to think, to act, and to behave are less diverse and more in line with a state's means of production and the greatly simplified economy that keeps wealth equal. To many of us, this again sounds like the old Soviet Union as far as *Eros* and family and friendships are structured.

Of course, as noted above, every family is unique, but the ideals of what a family ought to be is enforced, regulated, and corrected when any family gets out of line. While it is safe to say that parents love their children even under extreme socialist conditions, there is more trust among family members and friends, greater ability to reproduce with the many added welfare-oriented benefits of the state, and families can remain widely extended and unified. The only problem with this kind of ideal family structure and pattern deals with recognition and power within a circle of family and friendships.

No extremely socialistic state can avoid sibling rivalries for attention, for example, or avoid family members taking advantage of their parents' love. It is service to the state and the ideologies that radiate from within it that ensures power and recognition between family and friends. It has very little to do with materials or purchasing power.

For instance, if the state sends its citizens into war, they must all fight as a collective unit rather than a group of diverse individuals. This may seem the same in all military circumstances, but even though equality is stressed as well as cooperation and unity, there is still the division of power and recognition that must trump any notion of equality like the differences in rank and honor. In its place, we still have competition for power and recognition, but not for material goods. Therefore, if a son or daughter signs on for military service and succeeds at it, that son or daughter who is recognized by the state will get the most attention, praise, and even more power within the family. This is only one example, but there are many other examples in terms of labor as well.

Those who work harder, but not necessarily smarter or more efficiently, gain the most recognition, praise, and power by the state, and therefore, gain the most love from their parents and friends. As we can make out here thus far, there is still jockeying for greater reward even in the most ruthless societies that stress greater rather than natural talents that are indicative of a free market and a capitalistic society. The common link, though, is now obvious, and that common link is *Philia*. The love of family and friends is part of both extremes.

Of course, some family members may dissent and crave more freedom from the state in a socialistic world, but if they do this, they are more likely to be shamed, punished, and ostracized by their families, especially if they do not fall in line with pervasive state ideologies. Discipline of thought, discipline of belief, and rampant uniformity are hallmarks of the extreme socialist nation.

In democracies, we are lucky enough to hold both the concepts of freedom and equality as sacred and fundamental to any sort of advancement or national virtue, but when freedom and equality are so separated by political differences and partisan conflict, there cannot be a strong nation at all, as a nation becomes agitated by a war within itself. Two separate equilibria are formed, suggesting a split among the two fundamental concepts that democracy must have operating. This fundamental split is just too dangerous to ignore, not necessarily in socialist societies, which are more adept at keeping a nation's citizens together, but especially in raw capitalistic societies where the interference in the affairs of families and friendships is not enforced by punishment or the rule of law. It is instead enforced by religious bodies, ethical concerns, and money. Charity, moral behavior, and community service are stressed, but there is little or no punishment for the lack of these virtues, as the consequences in capitalism are just too weak.

One could argue that the functions and structures of families and friends within purely capitalistic economies reduce the power of the state and its power to dole out material goods and technological innovations. But it is economic success and economies of scale that lead to power and recognition and not loyalty to the state. Whoever has the most capital and whoever has the most purchasing power usually gets the most recognition and power those producers of goods and services that benefit the whole collective The gifts of social responsibility or even selfless heroism to the nation is only gained through capital and purchasing power. But social mobility through working smarter and not necessarily harder is made available to the many. A raw capitalistic society is highly competitive, as individuals must use their natural born talents. The goal is the procurement of more capital in order to survive and outpace the rate of inflation as well as the purchase more goods that are of greater quality. In other words, it's not collective labor or equal pay for equal work that is stressed, but who can climb a class ladder and gain all of the fruits of one's talents and not their arduous labors for wages that are kept low for the working poor or for those who must rely on the service economy. Citizens are free to pursue just about anything, just as long as the capital and the purchasing power exist to fund their own thoughts, ideas, adventures, and beliefs.

But this not as reckless as it seems, even though we could easily imagine and follow a through-line of thought to paint a dystopic portrait of raw capitalism. In technology and science there will definitely be greater innovation, yes, but only for those who possess basic technological skills, and mainly those who need or yearn for profit. Taxes are reduced for corporations and businesses as fewer public services are available for the least-well off, the poor, and the sick. This is a negative externality, yes, but this will be tempered by greater improvements in research and development of technologies that can alleviate some of the negative effects of raw capitalism. Even though the cable and satellite has replaced free broadcast television, the least well-off are still able to afford a digital antenna for obsolete television sets, for example, or even a television stick.

One can argue quite easily that the least-well-off have even more opportunity to develop in terms of their own natural talents, but only depending on the level of education, and the wealth one inherits. Education will be privatized and public education will be slashed for those who are unable to afford private education. There will definitely be higher quality in education, but higher quality for those who possess enough capital enough to pay for it. Better education will be available to those who inherit their wealth or possess higher natural talents. Natural talents and individuality will be stressed so that an individual will be able to break the barriers of social, psychological, and intellectual norms to join those who are the beneficiaries of inherited wealth.

Of course, wealth is no guarantee of success, but it forges connections to other elites and buys knowledge and technology. We can follow this line of thought to its very end, but we must also say that the major problem of capitalism in its rawest form is the growing divide between the very rich and the very poor. What we have, then, is the tendency for greater quality of goods and services that serve an elite few over the struggling disenfranchised. There is no regulation of wages, but only wages that are in line with the needs of economic elites who will enforce economic hegemony. We may indeed have a developing monarchy on our hands, and a once stable democracy that does away with equality will inevitably transmogrify into a kingdom stocked by inefficient royal members, or even a fascist dictatorship.

Many believe that this is actually beneficial to a society - to have decisions and laws made by fewer people than many. But this is also antithetical to any form of democratic governance. This scenario of raw capitalism, of course, is mere speculation, but it does lead us to some ideas of what a society may look like for families and friendships under conditions of *Philia*. We must stress that conditions of *Philia* still exist in raw capitalistic societies, but the greater the number of children, the lesser the level of love among and family and friends. What takes the place of the quantity and quality of friendships and family members is a sharp reduction in the number of children and family friends.

In sum, the farther down the class rungs we go, the fewer births and more nuclear families and friendships we will be able to have. To have a family and maintain close friendships and relationships will limit most of the population, as families will tend to become less gregarious, smaller, and more nimble and efficient to handle untethered inflation and depressed wages that must continue among the ever-deepening divide between rich and poor, the general erosion of the bourgeoisie, and the middle class. Those who have wealth and are talented enough to keep it will be members of an elite ruling class that will have to be forever wary of rebellion by the middle and lower classes that yearn for greater equality and greater fairness. The developing monarchy, then, will lead to the same tyrannies that caused these very democracies to form in the first place.

Within families, though, recognition by parents will come to high performing family members among working- and lower-class parents, but only if these working- and lower-class children perform services that please and benefit the elite at the lowest cost. The values of hard work will be stressed in such a family, but only if hard working high performers can withstand and tolerate dwindling wages and high inflation. Rebellion and conflict are bound to result, but these will be mostly among the young who realize how much the older generation and their older, oft-wealthier siblings work for fewer material goods and services - such as health care, access to medicine, and technology. This results in a type of stagnation for the young, but capitalism is such that there will always be the pursuit of greater materials and goods. There will always remain the distinct possibility that one could easily form a cooperative collection of individuals engaged making profit.

If a corporation does survive and profit, more employment is available, and a basic adherence to more microeconomic behaviors can be established among a community of corporations. But if a young person is neither interested in profit nor interested in having any social responsibilities that remind his or her society of the pursuit of profit as its primary social ideal, then punishment must fall by laws that favor the leisure and elite classes who have social responsibility by dint of how much profit they have gained.

For example, a law that is etched in stone is the singular individualization of the corporation. A corporation is seen as a single person with rights akin to an individual. No longer are they seen as a group that must be regulated as a group. If corporate monopolies are formed, there will be little pursuit by legislative bodies to enforce anti-trust laws that will benefit the many and diminish the power of an individual corporation in a capitalistic society. It is also safe to say that increased monopolies, amalgamations, and consolidations of corporations will lead to the domination of the working and poor classes and lead to a form of new-colonialism that imposes its power upon its own subjects.

But what is interesting here is that such raw capitalism cannot last very long, once families no longer have access to the quality of life now enjoyed by the elite few. It is almost like a form of apartheid that takes shape, and even though there are stiff penalties for protest and dissent, the many will always triumph over the few at some breaking point. Families and friendships will form that are governed more by capital and profitable pursuits than diverse interests and the presence of familial kinships and the level of trust needed to bind them together. There may be a diversity of opinion and belief that may or may not support the rule of these elites, but poor families will die off. Elite families will multiply and thrive in quantity but not necessarily by family quality. Once the gene pool of elites become limited to those with more equal and comparable talents, there will again be the stratification of those who succeed and those who don't. Elite families will begin to fight with other elite families of like-mindedness and wealth, repeating a cycle of class division that the elites had tried to spare themselves from in the first place.

So, we can say that there is greater competition within families and among friends and very little trust within these family and friendships. The rewards for competitive and more efficient acquaintances can be great and lucrative, even though what we have now is a democracy that is more unstable, even when there is a dominant ruling elite enforcing their own laws, simply because there is little or no *Philia* to bind people together. This can be seen as Social Darwinism in its rawest sense, a cruel but necessary function of the evolution of the species, because class struggle will then dominate these elites eventually - a never-ending cycle of implicit warfare, in a sense. Families will still be more interested in basic survival than the comforts and pleasures that a society with greater stability and greater. Intellect will matter much less as well as ethics and religion, while basic survival is enhanced and natural selection generates a more capable, stronger, and intelligent species. Every family member and their friends will want luxury but will always have to deal with brute survival blocking their paths to fuller lives for themselves and those they care about.

But *Philia* still exists, and familial love and love between and among friends and relationships that are close will always exist but only based on mutual interests, similar psychologies, and goals that are more in line with mutual survival and profit making. In socialist societies, especially at the extremes, families and friends experience a deeper more intrinsic love with greater quantities of people, but they are less likely to survive as well as in a raw capitalistic society. A socialist family may have a greater level of love and trust to enhance their lives but a capitalistic society places its emphasis on modes of survival and the skills needed to survive and compete in order to perpetuate the lives of the fittest, as the goal soon becomes survival by becoming the fittest. The capitalist human being survives but must suffer from a host of insecurities until the fear of death and destruction is abated by the development of greater skills and talents that allow him or her to live longer but not necessarily live happily.

Another important point can be stressed here. Extreme capitalist societies are more motivated by fear, and extreme socialist societies are more motivated by the unknown qualities of love as it relates to superstition, spirituality, and magical thinking. The people of the old Soviet Union, for example, believed in the brotherhood and sisterhood of love, but only a form of it that they did not have any empirical evidence of. In fact, it is well-known that such mysteries and superstitions were prohibited when the Soviet Union formed for the first time. While there were still many scientific investigations and advancements into these unknown mysteries and superstitious beliefs, these were mostly banned in favor of less spiritual, paranormal, and atheistic stances. The Soviets practiced a form of love, but in no way did it have any basis in faith, religion, or belief in God. It was a type of love that was a form of collective comradeship that denied the deeper mysteries, opportunities, and beliefs of spiritual and religious forms of love. So, while in extreme socialist societies like the Soviet Union love still exists, but love isn't as deeply nuanced and formed. It is a shallow type of love that stresses comradeship in the struggle to break free of class divisions. Nevertheless, even though love did exist in the Communist state, the Soviets were, of course, unable to measure it by scientific proof or atheistic fact, and so it was never plausible that love could evolve into a higher form of love that capitalist societies can more readily afford.

In extreme capitalistic societies, fear and paranoia are motivations that propel families to bond and continue their existence. In extreme socialist societies, love exists among family and friends, but it only exists in a very superficial form. Nevertheless, both motivations for human beings in both extreme systems of government and economy, both the fear in extreme capitalism and the undeveloped forms of love in socialism do still involve a higher and stronger version and vision of love that embraces both equally important and both equally volatile motivations that are only delivered through love's mystery. To avoid extremism within democracy, then, it is vital for both extremes to rely on the mysteries of love that they both share in common, even if this love is merely within those who are a part of separate extremes.

In terms of *Philia*, both societies love their families and friends, but just in different ways. Therefore, we can conclude that there is the same link in terms of common *Philia* between extreme capitalism and extreme socialism. And in order for *Philia* to link the two polar opposites, both libertarian and communist philosophies must co-exist and share the same space, let's say, but only through a democracy that guarantees certain inalienable rights as well as relies upon the mysteries of love.

We are not yet advanced enough as human beings to measure this higher, more ethereal form of love. But a higher form of love does exist in both extremes of government and are only able to function through the principles of a society that abides by democratic principles.

In terms of family and friends, then, it is the enlightenment and privileges that democracy provides and the mystery and existence of a higher love that guarantees both freedom *and* equality at the same time and within the same space. And love in democracy should not be confused with motivations for the basic need to survive, on one side, and the nascent, undeveloped forms of love established by recognition and hard labor, on the other.

In strong democracies, both freedom and equality must share the same space at the same time or else suffer division and, perhaps, self-destruction. That self-destruction among families and friends begins with the denial of the higher forms of love that give rise to this self-destruction. We can conclude here that *Philia* can only be sustained by an adherence and a strong belief in democratic principles and the higher forms and mysteries of love which family and friends already share in common. It is the link of democracy and higher love, then, that connects both extreme political realities, if and only if, democracy is still a principle worth saving. *Philia*, then, is more a result of a democracy and love, rather than a raw capitalistic society, a blatantly socialistic society, or any such world without love as its binding force, especially when it comes to family and friends.

Agape

The interesting quality of *Agape* is that this last kind of love on Plato's list that had been intently practiced and strongly advocated by Dr. King is most likely the most important of all of the forms of love that we have. Plato tried to prove the existence of this near-irrefutable philosophy and categorized these major types of love, but it was really Dr. King who put *Agape* into deft, and dare we say, brilliant practice.

It also helped greatly that Dr. King was able to use a dramatic reinterpretation of Christian text to bolster and fortify, on a moral basis, the support of white moralists, supporters of Civil Rights, and many more Christian sympathizers in the southern states. We should also be reminded of the white Jewish community's essential support of Civil Rights both in theory and in practice. Without Jewish support and identification with Black-American struggles, the Civil Rights movement would have never been successful. Jewish apathy or absence would have made a dramatic difference in the efficacy of the movement.

Islam's main appeal, at first, was to Black Nationalists, but once its leadership tested the waters of more traditional forms of Islam, many Muslims in the United States rethought their support of the Black Nationalist movement and moved closer to traditional Islam and the peace and love for all that it preached.

The rise of Black-Americans during the Civil Rights Era had to include all three monotheistic religions as well as the support, or at least the cautious observations and attentions, of the Far Eastern religions as well, such as Buddhism, to name one example. If we are extreme capitalists or extreme socialists, we cannot deny that all religions in the United States, and even our ardent atheists, all played important roles in the success and efficacy of the Civil Rights movement. No one would deny that.

The rise of Democratic Socialism, and to a lesser degree the socialist extreme of Communism, also played roles as well in developing the discourse that at least gave birth to Civil Rights and greater equality for all men. One example of this influence is the writers and thinkers of the Black Renaissance that predated the Civil Rights movement as well as those white intellectuals who learned from and encouraged this new and extraordinary wave of black thinkers, writers, and artists.

Extreme capitalists may have rejected the Civil Rights movement at first, but they at least had the hindsight to embrace such a movement as beneficial to extreme capitalist economies and the politics that supported extreme capitalism by creating a greater number of workers that would accept low-wage Black-Americans in corporate workforces. Of course, capitalism, in this sense, played more of a role in exploiting these workers at first, but capitalist thinkers were forward-looking enough to admit that greater numbers of low-wage workers would at least provide some benefit to the Black workers they exploited. Over time, Black workers would greatly benefit their corporations and the prosperity of all corporations, thereby paving the way for more diversity in occupations for Black-Americans and also higher pay that would successfully beat the rate of inflation in terms of benefiting the working poor.

But there are problems and grey areas when it comes to extreme capitalism as relating to struggling and poor Black-Americans and their neighborhoods. For example, (and this is to take a more obvious example that has riddled Black communities in the past), many businesses, such as chain stores and shops, both large and small, that enter poor Black neighborhoods, mostly due to subsidies and incentives by local and state governments that hope to improve deteriorating communities, will often charge prices much higher to those same stores and store owners that operate in the wealthiest of white neighborhoods. They offer their products at a much lower cost on the whiter, wealthier side of the tracks. This has riled up many poor Black-Americans in the past who cannot go into wealthy white neighborhoods for reasons beyond their control to purchase goods and services that are of lower cost by white communities. Most in struggling neighborhoods don't even have adequate transportation to travel to white neighborhoods. Instead, they are coerced, in many ways, to pay higher prices for the same goods with incomes that are already strapped. This creates great income inequality that the poor and the struggling must endure. In the past, this has been a source of great conflict in the racial divide. Add to this the same disparity in public and government services, and we can see where this leads in the ongoing struggle for racial equality for both poor Blacks.

For years, this has been a sore spot for Black and even Hispanic communities. But even though this unfairness seems ubiquitous in even the most moderate conditions of capitalism, white business owners who own such stores and must govern these services through tax dollars, politics, and the like, argue vehemently that they are simply following proper business models to ensure that their businesses stay afloat. They will also vigorously argue that the costs of insurance and security for each store will push prices higher, thereby creating this cost disparity through no fault of their own. So, while local governments use incentives to lure these businesses into improving their neighborhoods with their stores, the persons living in these poor, cash-strapped neighborhoods, are hardly benefiting at all. There may be a greater selection of products, but at higher prices no one in their right mind is able to afford them. And stores and small business that do not make enough of a profit to justify their stay in poor neighborhoods, can only pick up and leave, as the laws of business simply demand. These leaves vacant craters where businesses once were.

What this all suggests is that it takes elements of both the extreme capitalism of corporations and business owners and the extreme socialism of the services and protections that the state provides to promote effective and positive social change. It takes the cooperation and agreement of capitalists and socialists, whether implicit or explicit, to throw off unfairness, gross negligence, injustice, and immoral behaviors, unless those who are responsible are willing to face the full force of the reaction that follows.

After Dr. King's completely novel reinterpretation of the Christian faith, even most Southerners who had strong economic and political stakes in Jim Crow segregation and discrimination also had to agree that Dr. King at least had more moral authority than they ever did. What we can conclude, then, is that it takes at least some cooperation from extreme opposites over an issue, even among those who possess extreme and even unpalatable ideas and philosophies, to advance our nation and enhance both freedom and equality for all.

But this advancement through the cooperation of extreme and polarized opposites does not necessarily begin with explicit forms of injustice or unfairness, even though more empirical evidence of injustice, discrimination, and unfairness does contribute to the rise and exigency of such important advancement. What it must take, however, more than any one thing, is the love provided by Agape, or the love that comes with understanding. Without understanding, even the forms of love embodied in *Eros* and *Philia*, while always present and always available, are usually ephemeral and too nascent to form healthy and stable relationships among people and near and close relatives and friends.

What is interesting too is that it is even possible to speculate that there is a rational ordering and prioritization of experiences for these three types of love, and what is even more telling is that all three operate at the same time.

Certainly, most individuals experience all three forms at different levels and at different stages of their lives, but we must admit that the permutations of its functions, as well as the gradations of its presence and practices among all members of our nation are infinite and cannot be adequately measured. We do not yet know these levels nor how they interact and at what stages in our lives they appear, as these are either still unknown or simply unknowable. Again, this is love's mystery.

We have to stress here, though, that more than any one particular form of love, it is *Agape* within the volatile conditions of polar political extremes that is the most important and fundamental type of love, in a nation that must survive internal existential threats. It doesn't necessarily mean that a nation will be happy, prosperous, free, and healthy. It simply means that the country will be able to survive even through the most volatile, vitriolic, and chauvinistic civil discourse and unrest. It is the love of understanding of one another, and even groups of others, that must operate in order to ensure national stability and its existential continuance.

In sum, and as Dr. King wrote, a citizen of this country does not have to love or even remotely like another citizen. But both of these citizens cannot survive and a nation cannot remain together if these citizens do not have any capacity to understand each other's points of view or beliefs. The same goes for people of different races, colors, and creeds who, as individuals, groups, and whole neighborhoods, share the same communities or are in proximity to one another.

And there are three major qualities of a human being, who is either torn apart, on one side, or supported by, on the other, both warring, opposing, polarized, and extreme theories or political philosophies on how best to survive and prosper within a democracy. These three qualities and necessities are knowledge, empathy, and faith. When we speak of *knowledge*, we are talking about education. When we speak of *empathy*, we are talking about the ability of every man, woman, and child to put his or herself within another person's shoes for as much or as little time as he or she can. When we talk of *faith*, we must have an implicit or explicit belief that this country can work, just as long as we have faith in ourselves, at the very least, or faith in some kind of higher or even celestial force that will keep this country from splitting apart, just as it did in 1862.

Without *Agape* and these three qualities of human being is within each human being, we really can't have a united country. We instead will have a country in chaos and always on the brink of fissure and self-destruction. This destruction will be our own faults and not anyone else's. Let's take an idea that we can explore in terms of both public and private education.

Lately, the trend has been to have younger students study financial literacy in their basic curriculum. In these classes, the teachers discuss the nuts and bolts of money management, the role of investments, and wages for different careers. This is a very practical idea that was never taught in both public and private schools before.

Similarly, the literature of other cultures had never been taught in public or private schools to those of older generations especially. This all changed, of course, with the introduction of multiculturalism and the importance of studying all of the many cultural forms of literature for greater empathy and greater understanding among the young.

During the Post-Civil Rights Era, there was some slight movement to include some black literature within private school English classes, for example, but in no way did this small selection of Black Literature ever instill an ongoing sense of empathy, whether you were a black or a white pupil in an English class. It may have created certain reactions and feelings towards Pre-Civil Rights migration to the North, let's say, but it did not instill very much empathy at all among these pupils.

A solution to this would be to have younger generations of students take classes on cultural knowledge and sensitivity. For example, through a year-long course, taught by someone who is knowledgeable about the many different cultures that live here, the many diverse students in school can learn about the many different cultures, and more importantly, the cultures of his or her fellow students in the class. Students could inquire as to what other cultures believe and think, and this would also include white students who would inquire about those with different backgrounds to heighten their knowledge and understanding of difference better than a few books on Black Literature in a Junior English class ever can. We can make this a part of every school curriculum, whether that school is public or private. What we don't need is the separation of schools based on political ideology, race, faith, or creed. School choice can be a good option for parents and their children, just so long as courses, like financial literacy and cultural sensitivity, are part of their curricula.

Of course, it would be wrong to force schools to do this, but at least we can make it an enduring educational standard that reflects only the best of what American education has to offer. Financial literacy is just beginning to be taught, and cultural sensitivity courses are already being taught in contemporary education. Other courses for both public and private schools can also be explored.

For private schools, not only would financial literacy and cultural sensitivity courses help, but also a simple cooking course, which public school students already enjoy. Similarly, courses such as wood-working and journalism can teach students, not to instill them with greater knowledge in more traditional ways as students, but to give students real-life experiences in the real world, which many private school students will have to grapple with eventually. All of this is possible, if courses with both capitalistic biases and courses with liberal or socialist biases are taught within the same space. These courses need not be so explicitly biased, though.

In prior eras, it was mostly the teacher who held such biases and instilled them within their students, whether for good or for bad. But courses like financial literacy would benefit fierce capitalists, courses on cultural sensitivity, perhaps, would have a more socialistic bias, but still centrist And then there's woodworking, a practice that stresses the importance of trade unions in the wider socialist world. It is vitally important that such courses occupy the same space to give the student a broad education, not only for success in college, but for the larger world after his or her education is complete. Education, then, is essential to having knowledge if a student is to apply his or her own knowledge to the demands of practical living, not merely the larger and loftier ideas that are being taught at the college and university levels.

Empathy is also an essential component of *Agape*, and therefore, an essential component of any democracy that hopes to remain intact, and in the case of the United States, unified and properly functioning. Government representatives, as we have it now, are unable to empathize with anyone but those able to elect them and the donors who fill their re-election campaign coffers. Enablers include donors, political activists and action committees, large corporations, the wealthy elite, and perhaps some of their general constituency. Our binary system of government is mostly to blame for our dysfunction at the moment, but this will be discussed later. What we can remember, however, are the few leaders in recent American History who have had immense empathy for the entire citizenry of our nation and not just their own interests, their own electoral base, and in their own re-election. We will take the examples of President Jimmy Carter, on the Democratic side, and President George H. W. Bush on the Republican side. It is both extremely important to note here that both presidents failed to secure a second term, and we will argue here also that this is mostly because they considered the welfare of the whole of the nation as more of a priority than merely catering to either their Democrat or Republican states, respectively. Both presidents showed an incredible amount of empathy and tried to unite traditional conservatives and traditional liberals under the banner of democracy, and most importantly, in terms of the present day, tried to cobble together a unity that kept most citizens from vitriolically and vehemently disagreeing on nearly every matter of political policy and legislation as we are doing now.

It is widely known that while the traditional Republicans usually excel in foreign policy, they are weak when it comes to domestic policy. On the other side, Traditional Democrats are very strong when it comes to domestic policy, but notoriously weak when it comes to foreign policy. Presidents Carter and Bush are good examples of Presidents who possessed both of these strengths and weaknesses, respectively, but also as representatives of both parties to which they had to placate.

President Carter certainly had problems with both domestic and foreign policy. The OPEC Oil embargo in the late-1970s dragged this nation into a terrible recession, as we also found ourselves with high inflation. This definitely had many negative effects on the whole of society. But the other major reason for his inability to be re-elected was the infamous Iran Hostage Crisis and the removal of the Shah of Iran from power in Iran. What we received in return was the fiercely Anti-Western Ayatollah Khomeini. As a result, because President Carter had to allow the Shah's entrance and safe exile to the United States, he lost his re-election to President Ronald Reagan. For mostly moral and ethical reasons as well as reasonable political ones. What is hardly discussed anymore about President Carter is that through our intense and somewhat unprecedented problems with the Middle East, he was somehow able to forge an enduring peace between the Jewish nation of Israel and the Muslim state of Egypt. This was seen as an impossibility by most citizens, and yet we are now so fortunate because of it.

From detailed reports at the time of the historic Summit at Camp David, both Israeli leader Menachem Begin and Egyptian leader Anwar Sadat couldn't even stand to be in the same room together let alone be stuck in the same compound with the ability to hold meetings together. And yet through a tireless struggle by both President Carter and his fatigued staff, this outlandish administration was able to cobble together a peace treaty that still exists and stands today.

Granted that the rise of religious fundamentalism and internal politics within both countries *on both sides* have brought these two countries more apart in recent years, but President Carter, instead of offering the arrows of war, simply offered the olive branch of peace. With the intention in mind of securing the peace for both conservatives and liberals, he lightened the load of strife in the Middle East and while establishing greater security for the whole of our nation, sacrificed his domestic policies and his own re-election in return. We must remember that he was a one-term President who labored and competed hard for his re-election but ultimately lost.

The same kinds of values and ethics of President George H.W. Bush also made his presidency fundamental to the whole of the people and not just his party and his constituents who supported his re-election when he ran for a second term. He also was a fierce competitor, but he had to lose out to compromise domestically and also secure post-Soviet Cold War peace as far as his foreign policy was concerned. He also was a one-term president, but quite arguably, his presidency brought lasting benefit to the sum and not just its self-interested parts.

It was painfully clear that he vowed never to raise taxes before he was elected into office. "Read my lips," he said forcefully. "No new taxes." The crowd at the RNC erupted, and the nation followed suit. He held firm on this policy, but for the good of the nation, and not for his own popularity, he reneged on this promise and had to raise taxes to appease an opposing Congress.

President Bush had to compromise, not for himself or his party, but for the greater good. As a result of this, and we can argue that much of that was due to the reversal of his campaign promise, he lost the people's trust, and his own party turned its back on him. Secondly, just as the economy began to recover through his hard work, a Savings and Loan scandal rocked the nation, sending warning signs of yet a second recession and warnings of a run on the banks, as though a depression were possible.

The Reagan Administration also never intended for market prices to take a nosedive so precipitously. And even though President Bush inherited the mess and the difficult responsibility of cleaning up the whole of it during a painfully long recession and his hard work during this terrible drought and scandal paved the way for the election of President William Jefferson Clinton who was arguably one of the most popular presidents in American history.

But what could have otherwise been the pillage and rape of the post-Soviet Union had been skillfully diffused by the Bush Administration and his master negotiator Secretary of State James A. Baker. Instead of the need to imperialize the new Russian Federation, the Bush Administration resisted the urge to do just that and instead tempered it to a level that ensured peace and stability for a greater democracy in the new country.

Many in the United States as well as in Western Europe were certainly not in agreement, especially after trillions of dollars were spent on NATO's defense and many, many lives were sacrificed during this tense and deadly period of Cold War. But Bush had to go against the grain here and sacrifice this impulse for the greater good of Western Civilization as well as the new Russian Federation. Through James A. Baker, he also gained the trust of Arabs in the Middle East who were calmed to such an extent that they actually trusted America to broker more advanced and secure deals towards the ultimate goal of Middle East Peace. Baker especially made new overtures to Saudi Arabia, a process that began with Reagan, while securing greater security for long-time American ally, Israel.

Granted, both Presidents Carter and Bush were by no means perfect Presidents. But we can see, at least through this short summary, that the impact on the people they had placed under their governance was the first priority and leapt far ahead of their own self-interests. They understood that people more so than the other presidents, are much more important to the survival of the country. It is also interesting to note, that even though many liberals saw Bush as a threat, his idea of having "compassion" and "a kinder, gentler nation," did touch a rare nerve among even the fiercest liberals. If we remember our Norman Mailer, and we will paraphrase here, 'conservatives see the whole animal. Liberals only see the nice parts.' We can clearly see that Bush appealed to both. Sometimes, our best Presidents are never re-elected for this plain reason.

What followed was the Presidency of William Jefferson Clinton who had to improve the economy, not only because of the long recession during Carter or the slow recovery during the Bush Presidency, but also because of the widespread lack of confidence towards that a majority of Americans had towards the domestic inadequacies of the

Democrats, such as high crime, poverty, and their complete failure on bread-and-butter issues.

Clinton had to succeed with the economy, and his administration as well as his supporters knew this full well. But most of all, he had to give voice and energy to the stifled, more extreme elements of a liberal wing that had once given spark and lighted the fires of the Civil Rights Movement, the turbulent Anti-Vietnam War Movement, and the continuing battle for Women's Rights and an emerging, more mainstream Feminist and Gay Rights movements..

Wall Street simply had to shrug its shoulders and support a Counter-Culture, a Rock and Roll Revival, and a thriving Arts comeback as the greatest economic expansion in the history of the country at that point in time took firm hold and lasted until the final years of Clinton's presidency. From the clandestine bowels of the Department of Defense, the Internet had been fed to the mainstream public, creating an entirely new world of digitized information and global connectivity. Globalization and NAFTA became national priorities, and while many braced for the other shoe to fall, it never really happened soon enough, just so long as Clinton was at the helm and Congress played along. Even though most Americans knew that the kind of decadence in the 90s, the loss of family values, the recklessness of youth was bound to end at some point, it really never did. Until, of course, the stock bubble popped and sent overvalued technology stocks crashing. But for his time in office, Clinton delivered. The major problem, though? Clinton neglected the Midwest and Southern States that relied on the oil and national defense industries, agriculture, and the Armed Forces.

Globalization led large corporations to outsource their work to countries that promised cheaper labor costs, non-existent unions, and near-slave wages for low-income and slave workers. Manufacturing jobs and many blue-collar industrial workers here in the U.S. lost out to increased technological breakthroughs and immediate industrial automation and foreign cheap labor. Health Care costs soared.

Most in bleak rural communities looked askance at the poor and the unemployable who were given health insurance for free. No one particularly liked the idea of welfare either, especially for the criminals in the inner-cities who got away with theft and murder while collecting their hard-earned tax-payer dollars. No one should be given anything, they thought, unless they earned it through hard work, grit, and sacrifice.

It is interesting to note here, though, that the Armed Forces suffered the most under Clinton, as funding for the Defense Department and the military had been virtually wiped out, and morale among those in the services fell to record lows. A trend of families ruined by divorce, and children abandoned stark rural towns for urban opportunity and adventure. Family farms had been sold to large agricultural corporate powerhouses. The general corrosion of morality, discipline, optimism, and virtues among younger generations gave the impetus for the rise of Texas governor George W. Bush and the defeat of Incumbent Vice-President Al Gore.

To many who monitored this election, this was the closest election in history, and arguably the most important. In the end, it had to be up to the Florida Secretary of State, a female Republican, who predictably pushed Governor George W. Bush over the top to beat the Vice-President for the presidency by the thinnest of margins.

Many jaws dropped that day, but such was the election process. Many investigations of voter suppression and the lack of adequate voting technologies at the polls were conducted immediately. But George W. Bush won the Presidency, and the nation had to accept it to the silent applause and approval of those in the Midwestern and the Southern rural areas who had been totally and utterly neglected during the Clinton era. This is where the current extremism between a hard-driving capitalism and the rise of extreme socialism took place. A year into the Bush

Administration's uncertain governance came September 11th, 2001, the worst civilian tragedy in American History.

We are not going into this subject here, but let's just say that there wasn't a soul in America, or around the world for that matter, who wasn't affected by this tragedy. But again, let's save this for a later book, perhaps even a novel.

But to continue, by the Clinton Administration's neglect of a huge swath of American territory and the revival of the rural values of conservatism that was a reaction to old-time 1960s ideal liberalism. The pendulum had to swing far to the right, as many braced for a new large-scale war in the Middle East.

Bush did very well in preserving the balance between the left and the right, as this was extremely important, if not essential, for the preservation of the country, but most importantly he understood the fundamental right of every American to criticize him for entering a war that many argued was a terrible mistake in the year or so before the first bombings of Iraq began if they choose to do so.

What began as a brief incursion into the Middle East with the First Gulf War in Iraq by Bush I, Bush II renewed and expanded this short war that ultimately resulted in the complete and total conquest of Iraq, the assassination of its leader, Saddam Hussein, and the shift of the primary focus of the country towards the battle for a hard Christian Revival in

America against an antiquated, more fundamental form of Islam in the larger world, a battle that took place in the oil fields and deserts of the Middle East. It was clear to many, though, that such a war was inevitable, as the first signs of intense nationalism and growing discontent towards Muslims, even American Muslim citizens after the attacks, gained strength.

But Bush never stifled dissenting voices. Actually, most agreed that the United States needed to fight Islam in the Middle East, whether these Muslims were Islamofascists or not. Full support was given to the military and the Defense Department, and yet there were never any substantial cuts to essential social services, like Medicare and Social Security. Left and Right grew more extreme in their ideologies, yes, but at least they were able to share the same space, as the nation entered a phase of a long war that saw overwhelming popular support and approval.

This war, however, never seemed to end. Bush II won a second term, again by a close margin, as the majority gained confidence in his abilities to protect Americans from the Islamic threat, and as a paranoid public continued to support the defeat of Islam in the name of Christianity and Judaism, dissent against the War had been censored by most, if not all, media. Airtime dedicated to positive war coverage increased dramatically, and wartime tragedies on both sides were supplanted by stories of the heroism of US soldiers, police officers, firemen, and the first responders, and those who lost their lives in the September 11th attacks. The nation, once again, was unified by a common enemy.

And because President Clinton had signed a Crime Bill to gain even more support for his administration and prove to voters that Democrats could be as tough on crime as Republicans, a surge in the number of new generation police officers flooded the streets of urban centers, suburbs, and even small rural towns. This created a virtual police state within the country. Many believed Orwell is correct in his prediction.

But what matters most here is that once a much-needed Obama Presidency had been elected into office, yes, both extreme and traditional liberals were at least appeased in many ways, and the war in the Middle East still continued and grew in scope. It soon became a never-ending war.

And even though the Obama Administration did well, his presidency had to respond to crisis after crisis. In fact, many who look back may argue that the Obama Administration was really a crisis administration. Further acts of terrorism, the rise of the Isis threat in the Middle East, and huge natural disasters, like the flooding of New Orleans, endless hurricanes, tornadoes, and other nature-made havoc here in the United States and around the world, commanded the bulk of Obama's focus. And even though Barrack Obama, as many agreed, was a most capable President, and even though he succeeded as President in his two consecutive terms in office, many conservatives just did not trust Barrack Obama, especially when many of the Southern and Midwestern states that had just sent their sons and daughters to serve in a Middle East War, a war that never seemed to end, also held long-standing attitudes that never trusted a once-Chicago inner-city activist who may have had Islam somewhere in his family tree. He was the first Black-American president in the history of the nation, which didn't help them any. After Obama left office came the fierce extremism and fascist backlash of the radical right.

Donald J. Trump became the next president of the United States. He easily lost the popular vote narrowly won the Electoral College. And when he won, there were many on the left and the center, and even traditional Republicans, who questioned the legitimacy of the Electoral College as the vehicle for fair representational voting in the nation. The favorite by a long shot, Senator Hillary Rodham Clinton, the first viable woman candidate and also President Bill Clinton's spouse, lost the election despite widespread popular support and much more financial support. President Donald J. Trump took over the reins of office to everyone's surprise, and many feels, and perhaps even to his own.

Many independents and neo-Centrists have mixed views about the Trump Presidency. Both Traditional and Populist Conservatives are sticking together, and on the opposite side, so are unafraid intellectuals, powerful, money-rich Clinton Democrats, and most of the nation's disenchanted and frustrated youth. What's more, especially the working poor in urban areas of the nation are fiercely against Trump's re-election. But let's examine the role of the independent, disaffected voter and those who find themselves a growing part of a political center that first took shape after the September 11th attacks. We will define this interesting and fast-growing group as the political "Center."

The political center has mixed views about President Trump. First of all, this is a generation that is primarily middle age. They have benefited greatly from the economic surge during the Reagan presidency, the swift economic cleanup during the short-lived George H.W. Bush Presidency, and the incredible pampering of the populace and widespread ideological 1960s nostalgia garnered of the Clinton era. They may have championed the presidency of Barrack Obama as well, but to this particular group, President Trump poses more of a perplexity than a solution to any of the nation's problems or any of the successes he has had in his time in office thus far. What may be at the heart of these mixed views about President Trump is the ever-growing generational gap between the old and the young, and especially, the ever-widening gap between the wealthy and the abject poor and even the working poor.

From just a cursory investigation of this evolving group, the older generation of older baby boomers as well as older-aged World War II Veterans are living much longer and have amassed greater wealth than any other generation in the country at this moment. As of this writing, a *Huffington Post* article revealed that the real growing divide in America is between old and young and no longer between left and right. This is arguable, but at least it points to what a growing trend may be in the politics of the moment and perhaps and more importantly here, a loose definition of where exactly the center stands on more specific concerns and how they feel about President Trump.

As we mentioned, the Center has mixed feelings. They understand the President's success in his foreign policy, for example. This is primarily because he is willing to meet with these rogue foreign leaders and has developed a growing, iterated relationship with them instead of leaving such relationships in the hands of the military or the intelligence services, and a hawkish Democratic party that has somehow become the authority on dealing with enemy nations. What began with Dennis Rodman's 'basketball diplomacy' in North Korea now includes the full participation of President Trump and his foreign policy advisors. In foreign policy, President Trump may not be walking away with instant deals and results with despots, like Putin and Kim Jung Un, but at least he is willing to use 'soft power', just as President Clinton did, to show how America can bring these leaders out of their pasts and into the more luxurious American present. This appeals even to the most liberal of baby boomers despite their reservations.

To add to the Trump Administration's foreign policy advances, the addition of the openly and brazenly hawkish John Bolton as National Security Advisor was seen by some centrists as positive to our international position. Despite all of his politics and faults, Bolton has contributed to much of these foreign policy decisions. Add to this former-CIA Director and now Secretary of State Mike Pompeo, with his experience in foreign affairs and foreign governments, and the Trump team, when it comes to foreign policy, may lead many centrists to conclude is now on the right track, perhaps with the exception of President Trump's restrictive tariffs on imported goods from China and the slowing of economic growth here in the U.S. due to a trade war with a country that had once earned the country's most favored trading nation status.

Our relationship with Russia, though, has grown increasingly complex, but there is good reason to speculate that Russia and the United States may, in fact, be colluding in very subtle ways to the mutual benefit of both countries. There is little or no hard evidence to support this, of course, but there are subtle hints that this may be happening.

For example, military cooperation is continually increasing, even though Russia and The United States appear to be on the outs diplomatically. 'War Games' between Russia and The United States closer to Russian territory ensues as both powers learn the strengths and weaknesses of their own Armed Forces. Similarly, Russia can no longer rid itself of its continued oligarchical dominance over its citizens and its government. Russian oligarchs have become so powerful that they are now a functioning part of the Russian economy. A return to old Soviet-style Communism is highly unlikely, though. Also, most of the oligarchs who have now accrued mass wealth after the fall of the Soviet Union, also vigorously support Putin and his rise to power. So even though there is the Western accusation of despotism when it comes to Putin, the Trump administration will aid Putin in solidifying his power. By building up Russia and staging the growing distance between both of them at this time, the U.S. might be cooperating than we initially thought. This is because the rebuilding of Russia into a superpower compliments American interests as well.

Russia can benefit from America tremendously, also in terms of its military, technology, and intelligence methods. Secondly, just in terms of its commodities and resources, Russia is plentiful in oil and is more willing to trade with America at very low cost for it. Also, because Russia has a more balanced and calmer hand in the Middle East, it can advance American interests there by keeping all of these threatening countries on an even level of power, as Russia's foreign policy approach treats every country in the region with a much more delicate and tender hands than America ever did. And this can help America withdraw from the region when the time comes to leave.

There is, however, an idea in the mind of many analysts that deserves investigation. Through this subtle collusion between Russia and America, America hopes to build a very strong and capable Russia so that it may create and maintain a global duopoly. There will still be a dedication to socialism on one side and a dedication to a market economy on the other, but the joining of these two nations will bring a balance of power so that needless wars among smaller countries do not simmer on and break out into war.

This, of course, is all speculation, because there is very little evidence of this cooperation occurring. But there is evidence that suggests that the two nations can benefit from cooperation by chasing mutual interests. The ultimate goal may only be to establish a balance of power by staging an ersatz Cold War so that needless and much larger wars and conflicts, usually perpetrated by smaller and more unstable countries, are pleasantly avoided, not to mention the economic and financial benefits that are realized by both of them.

What also may appeal to centrists is Trump's defiance of prior policies of globalization. We have to remember that the industrial towns of the Midwest and even the Northwestern Rust-Belt have nearly vanished and have created new pockets of poverty for many rural poor and once urban poor who had at one time enjoyed a more meaningful culture and greater wealth in hometowns that are now dead. Even once-thriving cities like Amsterdam, New York, a place just forty-five minutes north of Albany have been reduced to low-income neighborhoods and small businesses. This is a direct result of vanishing industries that have moved elsewhere, either overseas or to places with more favorable tax rates and lower labor costs. Of course, large industries leaving towns is a common tale, but never before has the problem been more widespread. It has leveled once young and thriving populations.

As of this writing, Trump's relationship with China is of particular concern to many, if not all citizens, but this may be so, because President Trump is unable to articulate exactly why Chinese imports need to be taxed. The necessity of the trade conflict is poorly articulated and is framed within the fiery fascist rhetoric that appeals only to the worst impulses of his base. But neo-Centrists may come to the conclusion that the President is actually helping white working poor laborers by breaking labor unions who are perceived by corporations and Republicans in general as either fundamentally corrupt, an obstacle to free markets, or even the base of the Democratic Party.

What may also be speculated is that the current President is now combating the widespread dumping of cheap Chinese consumer goods and also goods from lesser-developed countries in the American marketplace, and is developing mostly white labor-oriented businesses that employ white working poor laborers, like construction workers, farm hands, and factory workers, who do not belong to labor unions or any kind of collective-bargaining organization. This helps the blue-collar, freelance economic operator, much like the Internet has helped the freelance white-collar worker that had been so championed and institutionalized by the Democratic Party.

But what is also obvious is that Trump's policies have given unbridled power and influence to large American corporations and have broken labor unions. While this may be sound business policy, as far as high profits and lower prices are concerned, it nevertheless pushes the costs of purely American labor into the free market as well, thereby making the cost of labor for every American worker as competitive as all workers in the country as it would for the fair compensation of cattle or corn or orange juice. Also, corporations are no longer required to pay higher prices for worker protections like occupational safety, healthcare, and worker's compensation, which would vary by state.

But his goals for cities like Amsterdam, New York, are usually met by most with confusion if not outright objection. While the President wants to expose laborers to free-market competition, corporations will only employ workers and develop their industries in states that do not have strong unions that mandate paying higher wages and worker benefits. Amsterdam is not a city that would benefit from President Trump's policies, and yet his fiery nationalist rhetoric still entrances the working poor in this neglected city who tend to support him. The actual economic gains, however, are realized by the Midwest and Southern states who have little or no union presence as well as those states that are not traditionally pro-union.

There are many more cities, just like Amsterdam, especially in the rural areas of the Northeast and the West. This trend of declining smaller cities, long ignored by the Washington establishment, have forced many of these residents to leave and relocate to urban centers or leave these once-wealthy regions totally and head to the cornfields or even the Bible Belt. This rippling effect typified by such demographic change puts great strain on pro-labor cities that do have strong union backing while they also absorb unemployed laborers who had been looking for work in poor, desolate towns where jobs were once plentiful.

But bringing back American manufacturing may have widespread appeal to centrists. An end to globalization as well. By resurrecting the status of the white working poor, Trump's America no longer has to outsource its hard labor to other countries. As a result, America would no longer have to protect other countries with their military, police, intelligence, and other police-worthy agencies just to protect American economic interests. If Western-oriented democracies follow suit, no longer would the United States have to be policeman to the world.

This idea also appeals to younger and more middle-aged people, as many of them grew up in times of peace and prosperity, fiercely opposed to any sort of war. They even support 'The New Feminism' during this difficult time for women. Baby-boomers taught them well about government over-reach, corruption, and prevarication, especially when it came to the war in Vietnam, the dangers of totalitarianism, and political oppression. We can arguably say that this same center is what is left of the bourgeois and the now-restless eroding middle classes. They are educated and informed, and even though we can easily dismiss them in a variety of different ways, this group will be the undecided, independent voters in this election.

But while Trump has succeeded in foreign policy, and many centrists also believe that he has succeeded on Wall Street and on unemployment as well, his domestic policies, his serious lack of any presidential character, and his unpresidential tweets and tirades, the growing concerns about his mental health and psychological stability, his militant, conservative brand of fascism, his tacit acceptance of white nationalism, and suddenly the ever-growing noose of corruption that threatens to squeeze the life out of his presidency are absolutely atrocious and, dare we say, despicable. It is also avoidable, had Trump been of good character to begin with. And even if neo-Centrists greet Trump's character with apathy or arbitrariness due to his performance on the economy and his defiance of the hard-won cultural institutionalization of political correctness and identity politics, his approach to politics is unwise, as he attempts to run the executive branch as a tyrannical CEO or wing-nut ideologue would. If this is the case, then that would make the President woefully politically naïve about all aspects about how a country ought to be governed.

Interestingly, all of the details and the implementation of his executive orders are made by advisors and cabinet members who can easily manipulate the President into writing any policy they care to implement. In sum, while the President may want certain deeds done on behalf of his base and the country as a whole, he may also be completely unaware of *how* they are being done and *for whose* direct benefit.

Like Reagan earlier, and President George W. Bush later him, the Republican Party may be using Trump as their mouthpiece. While he may be the one who directs his servants to "make things so," Trump's trustees and advisors may not be trustworthy at all, considering that they are more far-right in orientation and not traditionally conservative, as Richard Cheney is or James Baker was. Traditional conservative trustees are usually faithful to their Presidents, but whether or not Trump's trustees care and look out for the wellbeing of their President may not be the case at all. In fact, they may be using him for their own ends, whatever those ends may be.

What's more, it is hardly reported what is happening behind the scenes of his administration and what policies are actually being implemented, especially as most news coverage focuses on the findings of the Mueller Report and the looming impeachment crisis. His advisors may even be using their President as a convenient distraction while their own ends are being met and hidden from the mainstream press.

But to return to neo-Centrists and party moderates alike, many may be thinking in terms of domestic *realpolitik* that President Trump and his administration has the Brown Shirts but not the Intelligentsia just yet. Some may skeptically project that as a result of his dedication and fierce support of his base - mostly the white working poor and the values of the more rural and Sothern and Midwestern conservatives - he may go on to take advantage of his base's loyalty and use his popularity to redevelop these neglected rural areas using knowledge of real estate, thereby taking advantage of low-cost labor, manufacturing, and old world commodities like steel, coal, and oil, after his term expires. Some may envision the future of these rural and forgotten areas, totally neglected by the Washington establishment, as dominated by the business and financial interests of the Trump Organization.

Aside from the obvious hyperbole of this vision, the feelings and thoughts of this growing chorus of centrists about our current President as outlined here has mixed feelings, and therefore, more potential to harness the powers of *Agape* to heal the nation from its continuous political mood swings, never-ending strife, dangerous ideological divides, decades-old polarization, and an increasingly bellicose Millennial generational populism that will soon allow their voices to be heard during this upcoming election period. This is the main point of summarizing what past Presidents have accomplished and have not accomplished. Centrists have more power than ever before to shape the future of the country.

We must not confuse, however, the Center's political apathy or silence with having mixed-feelings either. Neither must we consider the Center to be without any sort of spine or backbone. We must now consider them as a powerful force in American politics. They are both experienced and educated enough to understand the dangers posed by the extremism of both capitalism and socialism. They are well aware of their mixed-feelings, and they are most likely the most knowledgeable among us they remain totally perplexed and confused in the same breath as to where the country has gone since the September 11th attacks.

Interestingly enough, the television commentator, Tucker Carson, in his well-known book, *Ship of Fools*, uses an idea that attacks our elite progressives as most populists would do in an age of strife. But no matter how anyone judges Tucker Carlson. the following quotation from his latest book actually highlights a lasting trait of Western Democracy that many centrists have already known within a much larger theoretical context.

> "Liberals were no longer giving peace a chance.
> If anything, by the 2016 presidential election, liberals
> seemed most agitated by the idea of not being in
> conflict with other countries. In one of those weird
> historical ironies that almost nobody seemed
> to appreciate at the time, the Republican in the
> race was running well to the left of his Democratic
> opponent on key foreign policy questions. Donald
> Trump gave speech after speech attacking the
> wars in Iraq and Afghanistan, and the idea of nation
> building more broadly. Hillary Clinton was still
> defending the decision to kill Gaddafi."

What are these *weird historical ironies that nobody seemed to appreciate at the time* exactly? Many centrists, who are often among the most disaffected voters in our nation already, know what these strange ironies are. Tucker Carlson also provides a clear example of it, although he doesn't mention it or may not know it yet.

Within our binary nation where two parties dominate and where a winning party must take all, there is a tendency to have the citizens of our nation switch sides. Some jump to the Republican side, because progressives get too strong. Some Republicans, who have had enough of Trump's rhetoric, will jump to the Democratic side. They have no choice. There is no center yet. There is no middle. Instead, they must choose one extreme or the other. In the end, it leads them towards the Center, where they are greatly prone to switching sides. While centrists are free to vote for anyone and any ideology, the only real winners in any form of democracy are the two dominant competitors, the left or the right. This is true of all Western Democracy, no matter how people struggle to cobble together a viable third party. Third parties are quickly rooted out, because they are simply spoilers. We know that already.

But we can speculate that this drastic switching of sides between the hawks and the doves, the student and the teacher, the master and the servant, is a quality of life as old as time here in the West. But no longer is it such a friendly and peaceful switching here in the United States. Many in our nation believe that President Trump is to blame for this unfriendliness and rife bellicosity. Our condition now threatens to break that essential political and spiritual trade that has been historically made between opposites. It is a gradual process, but it does takes place.

Yes, even traditional Southern Democrats, whom many had thought were so fierce in their Southern ties and loyalties, had to jump ship to the Republican side. 1960s Civil Rights Activists of yesterday, who so staunchly supported the party of John F. Kennedy, are now forming their alliances with President Donald Trump in keeping with their allegiance to the Christian church and their response to the 'gansterization' of urban areas of Black America.

Another example may be how Vice-President Al Gore and former Governor George W. Bush of Texas appealed to the entire voting public when they ran for President after Clinton's last term in office. Al Gore seemed to be a lot more intelligent than Bush, but while running for office, Bush stressed the importance of having good character and faith. Not only was instilling a sense of good character and faith one of the pillars of his campaign, it is also a long-standing traditional conservative principle. Those supporting Al Gore, however, thought Mr. Bush one of the most unintelligent presidential candidates ever to run for office.

In our country today, the complete opposite is true. The parties have completely switched sides. President Trump represents a corrupt politician who has an incredible criminal intelligence that the Democrats in Congress loathe. He has escaped their clutches on almost everything they have accused him of. Similarly, Democrats have never been the champions of good character and faith. Yet they feel they must stop a criminal president from abusing his power and using his position to divide the country.

This kind of criminal intelligence is exactly what Republicans couldn't stand about President Clinton. The Democrats couldn't stand how sanctimonious the Republicans were in pursuing, and then even impeaching, President Clinton over what many saw as immoral or even criminal behavior. The parties, at this time, have flip-flopped. For the American people, day has become night, and night has become day. All of us have to follow or risk the negative consequences of it, no matter what personal beliefs we hold or cherish.

Where would Dr. King fall along the political spectrum today? Are the Republicans really the party of Abraham Lincoln in this day and age? This is what we mean by these *weird historical ironies*. Is it a function of Christianity, or is it some other Godly force that causes this? No one can be certain of anything. Many simply know it exists, and in the West we are powerless to do anything about it, except perhaps, change our skins, abandon our political beliefs, or jump on the bandwagon, only to reverse our political beliefs for the beliefs we had previously when a switch must take place later down the road. Even those who are so entrenched in their political beliefs, whether extremely conservative or extremely liberal at the moment, must switch sides at some point, just like the Southern Democrat had to. Centrists simply have to go where the government tells them to go.

They have to adjust to new behaviors and to new laws enacted by whoever controls the Congress and whoever is elected into the Oval Office. But centrists are at least aware of it, and these are the same people who may now deliver this country from the mess we now find ourselves in. They alone may be the only alternative to our binary system, maybe not now but in the future. It is this same binary system of government that our founding fathers had baked into our very Constitution, whether they intended to or not, for better or for worse. This is what America wants from its allies and all of its citizens.

There are a few examples from past artists of all kinds that also illustrate the point. Let's look at a few of M.S. Escher's drawings that demonstrate this idea of switching sides, but not in anger or hatred, but in friendship and goodwill. Notice how he draws black and white birds transforming and changing into opposite colors *through* each other. Notice how these beautiful birds don't have to kill each other. The same example can be seen in another Escher drawing in which a circle of men, both black and white, must move *through* each other, and instead of fighting about it, they are shaking hands and smiling in cooperation as they transform into their polar opposite colors. These are the *weird political ironies* that makes Carlson's example so important, unbeknownst to him.

Elton John's song *Mona Lisa and Mad Hatters* also illustrates this exchange, and perhaps this is the only irony that keeps our Western Democracy in place. H.G. Wells' *the Time Machine* is also a testament to this process. Today, though, it remains to be seen who is forced to live underground and who gets to stay above ground and frolic in the sunshine, as many centrists have already observed. We can also cite other examples. Even though penned originally as a love song, Joni Mitchell's *Both Sides Now* also illustrates the point. We can even indulge in Hollywood films by citing Warren Beatty's *Bulworth* and its portrayal of the danger when an elected official attempt to fulfill American Democracy's true promise by learning and gaining support from both sides.

And here we are now. We are close to another point in American history where we could face either further capitalist extremism or a backlash that swings to the other extreme of socialism. But this time around, the threat of social unrest and staunch opposition to extreme conservative populism by those on the side of extreme socialism will inevitably lock horns. We are close to an election year, and, as many are now predicting, this may be the most vitriolic and violent election period since the nation's first and only Civil War that began in 1862. Both sides are strong and are willing to fight. And, as only a few may see at this point, it is this civil war and unrest that comes with rural, conservative brawn on one side, and more high-brow, urban and suburban, liberal brain on the other that threatens national security more than international terrorism does.

Such is the nature of our internal conflict of today. It is the same binary conflict between fuzzy logic and fuzzy math, Caesar's strategies and Socrates' philosophies, The Army of Sparta and The School of Athens, Ancient Rome and Ancient Greece, and finally, the heart and the mind. And to where does this binary conflict lead the American soul? All of the presidents before Trump, as discussed, already had it.

This does not mean to sound at all apocalyptic, because many of us can still use our knowledge and our empathy of both liberal and conservative extremes to intervene and prevent our country from going completely off the rails. But the only reason for this ray of hope at this time is our capacity to have faith, either in our human selves or any other kind of power or spirit greater than ourselves. Faith, then, is the final cornerstone of *Agape*. It is as equally important as the other elements of *Agape* discussed here.

There must be at least be some level of inherent faith within us as human beings or within some higher power, spirit, or force that we will come out of this period of extreme political tumult as we usually come out of it: with ourselves and our country intact, even though we may suffer injury, sickness, or death from it. Of course, this may not work this way in reality for most of us, but with faith more is possible than having no faith in anything at all.

Even the great atheist Ayn Rand, though she probably would have never admitted this to anyone openly, must have had at minimum some kind of faith or confidence that her theories on the threats of collectivism and the virtues of even the most extreme types of selfishness are plausible and acceptable despite any belief in a God of any kind. Actually, atheism, in general, and those who believe that any kind of supreme being or invisible, celestial force can in no way be proven in any sense, still must espouse some faith or rudimentary belief in their stance despite the overwhelming lack of popular support in this belief.

We must also note here that many atheists argue that if we look at objective reality, such as fierce competition, government totalitarianism, crimes such as murder, rape, theft, and also the many battles and wars that have maimed and killed millions in the name of some false deity or God, atheists themselves must somehow also espouse a fierce sense of personal ethics and morality that proves to them quite easily that the human being and what he or she has developed in terms of his own evolution, like the scientific method and science in general, is far more superior to any sort of higher spirit or God that may exist.

Interestingly enough, many atheists look within themselves to find distinctly human talents that can carry them through life or existence, such as strong ethics, intelligence, natural talents passed on through generations and experience, and a wisdom not delivered by any kind of God or Prophet but through their own innate abilities and through other developments that neither involve any higher force nor powers other than themselves or the groups of people who will one day be devoured by the soil or preserved cryogenically for regeneration in later centuries.

Yet even though they do not believe in any sort of higher power or force operating in the world, the atheist still has faith that he or she is right and correct and can operate much better than any direction offered by any conception of God that gets in the way of his or her life. But faith is still there within the atheist. Faith in democracy is there is as well. Most importantly, faith in his own country is present, even though there may be very small traces of it or a very large presence of it. We cannot deny it any longer that atheists must too have some faith, whether in our presently extremist nation or in themselves as human beings.

Most in the world who are not atheists, however, believe in a Higher Power, and the number of these people, the level of their faith, and the rituals they practice are dizzying to say the least. Agnostics are also numerous, but they also have faith in good outcomes despite their doubts in any God or other higher forces directing these outcomes.

Faith in God, though, should interest us greatly, especially during times of extreme political stress on our economy or our lives during times like these. There currently is a fierce battle, not only between those who believe in God and those who don't, but also the many and ever-growing religions, both large and small, that find themselves lost in this wilderness of these ever-growing extremes on both sides of the political divide. Religious issues have emerged at the forefront of fundamental policy debates on how individuals ought to be governed and how society ought to function. The debate has become so fierce, that it will remain an important and contentious issue for many years to come.

Many of us, for example, are aware of the question of whether or not a child has the right to live, or whether or not this child's mother has the right to choose whether or not this child has to die before this child is born into our world. This is just one example of an issue that may never be resolved in our country nor the world for that matter.

We must acknowledge, though, that both arguments are perfectly valid. They just exist on different planes. The first, the pro-life argument, basically argues that life begins at conception, and that science has even proven this. Also, the termination of pregnancy is an act that goes against God's command or wishes for those who worship him, her, or even it, or whatever that God may be. Also, for those who often cite the many scriptures within religious texts, this is in direct disobedience of God's will, and abortions must be stopped immediately. Therefore, God's people and those who interpret religious texts in a more literal sense must protest and fight as much as they can, whether peacefully or even to another extreme, violently to make sure that God's will is preserved.

For many women who believe that a woman has the right to choose, the argument is much different. This is not because they believe or do not believe in a God or a religion. This is mainly because in a democracy such as ours it is the fundamental right of the woman to decide what she does with the child growing inside of her, no matter if it is an embryo that is in question or the child who is more developed. Some even take the rarer view that a woman should be allowed to choose no matter the age of the child before that child is born, even when the pregnancy is late-term. What is at stake here is not God or any kind of spirituality, but the fundamental right to choose and the right to be treated as equal members of our functioning democracy as guaranteed by the Constitution.

They imagine a country where the state even governs their own womb, crippling their chances of any sort of equality or any sort of say or governance over their own bodies. So many women have at least some religious or spiritual faith and that this has never been a question of a belief in any God at all. The argument, instead, is over the equal rights of women and the power to choose in a democracy that has long denied their rights to take part in the democratic process. They see that that the right to govern their own bodies and their own children is fundamental to this equality. In this light, women also have a valid point, just like those who follow the commandments and the wishes of God with their literal interpretation of scripture.

What we have at the present time, though, is a growing and very young feminist group who is willing to use any form of protest, including violence, to have their way. This is also similar to their opposition, who is against abortion of any kind. The point here is that once again most of the nation is governed by extremes. There seems to be no compromise where compromise ought to be. Such extremism on both sides has to be brought into the middle ground by those who have faith in a democracy where compromise has always been the norm.

127

Both pro-life and pro-choice women who share the same space, the women who side with God and the women who have faith in the equality of women, and want the government out of their very own bodies still have to have faith that compromise will be struck and that compromise, whatever that may be, doesn't have to involve anger or even vitriolic debate or even violence to make their arguments heard. Compromise is the key here as well as faith in the democratic process. And since women already have faith in their beliefs and positions, there must also be faith in their willingness to compromise for the benefit of the nation. Banning late-term abortions, for example, which is already the law and is widely agreed upon by most women, is one such compromise. Supporters of pro-life policies must also take a step towards them. This is the way it works, not through all-out binary politics at all times.

Take another such argument that riddles most of us. The conflicting ideas of God and Science. Stem cells and genetic engineering and even in-vitro fertilization are always under dispute by creationists. Even adoption, in some religions, is seen as a violation of God's will. In Islam, in particular.

But a lot has changed since the Scopes Monkey Trial. Scientists had to employ the scientific method to prove that anything existed at all. To prove that God existed, many religions had to refer back to religious texts and the presence of things unknown and unknowable. But it is hard to deny that many scientists are also men and women who believe in God. What ethics does for science, morality does for religion, and vice-versa. And although many scientists acknowledge that they are able to include both God and the rigors of science in their own lives, the divide has still become deeper and more sophisticated.

There have now been advances in creationism and creation science which many contemporary scientists would call 'magical thinking.' Also, many creationists would argue that their findings stick to similar methods of discovery but scientific discovery is usually handled unethically and immorally. Yet, sides will have faith in their positions, and most creationists and most scientists will probably need the doctors or the hospitals at some point. Similarly, most scientists will still have faith that science itself and the many advances that will come in the future will bail humanity out. Either that or the technology that spawns from scientific advancement will be used to kill many by no intention of their own, like the Atomic bomb. This is where *Agape* comes into play in all of the cases that we've discussed.

All divides require education, empathy, and faith to bridge them. The same with the extremes in capitalism and extremes in socialism. The evolving nature of our society has put us in this unique position. Even the interpretation of our own Constitution has changed dramatically. Everything we read and everything we interpret from the information we are given from books, textbooks, and media has also changed. We now have a divide between the literal and the figurative interpretations of our own Constitution. This is yet another reason for the divide to grow even more extreme.

Let's take gun control, which is an issue of importance at the forefront of many political debates. The Second Amendment of the Constitution is at issue. Many will take this particular amendment literally. "The Right to Bear Arms" is a literal right etched in a static Constitution that doesn't change and ought to be literally interpreted. Others will argue against this and say that the Constitution is an evolving document which can be interpreted in an infinite number of ways by all Americans, as all Americans have an equal right to their own ways of interpreting any text, and the Constitution is no exception.

Many historians will argue, for instance, that the Second Amendment is often taken out of context, because at the time of its ratification, it only applied to state militias that needed to defend themselves against a powerful federal government. The Right to Bear Arms was not a right, originally, for the general public to revolt against any kind of state or local authority. Proponents of gun rights, however, will say that the only way to defend themselves against the tyranny of any government's if it does not serve the needs of its people, whether that government is a local, state, or federal one. This fundamental right to bear arms is literally granted in the Constitution. And while this debate still rages and polarizes the nation, any inch given away will be seen as the other side taking a yard, and this is a major problem. There exists a skewed view that there is a zero-sum game between the two sides that is being played in all of this.

Either one side wins, or one side loses. It is either 1 or 0, 'off' or 'on', this or that, either-or, and so it goes. Again, there has to be a faith in compromise that arrives at a fairness that all Americans can live with, regardless of what permutations these positions take. Forms of protest should always be allowed to take place, as that is a fundamental part of any democracy, but we must also have faith in the powers of compromise, no matter to what extremes these conflicts and debates have pulled the entire nation. Again, both are right and both are wrong, and the only solution to any kind of political paradox such as this is time, patience, and the willingness to compromise and work together to solve difficult problems. In the case of gun control, more bipartisanship may be helpful and not necessarily a mass election that may put an already anxious and struggling population on an even worse footing than before.

We can discuss any number of issues that are sized up exactly like this, but what they all share in common, however, is the knowledge and belief that we will still survive as a nation no matter what. This is yet another form of faith.

Interestingly enough, though, a novel form of protest was held at the news conferences of both Attorney Roger Stone and the Attorney for the defendant Paul Manafort, both men accused of a slew of white-collar crimes while they were in the Trump Administration. A youngish slender man wearing a tuxedo and a long, red wig of hair held up a large cardboard sign that read "This is a Sign" for the media cameras to see. This is an example of a solution to how we may be able to bridge these incredible divides. "This is a Sign" can be interpreted both literally and figuratively *at the same time*. It wasn't a form of protest so much as an appeal for a way to find compromise and to find solutions to our most difficult problems. It was artfully done, and at least as of this writing, the man's point was well-taken.

And yet, despite all of these divides, we are still stuck with a binary form of government. A plurality of thought doesn't work right now, but *Agape* can bridge any divide, even in our systematically-flawed binary system. If we are willing to use the ideas of *agape* and implement them towards the public good, whatever forms they may take, we may be able to overcome our difficulties.

There will always be ideas that we don't like and find debatable, deplorable, or even downright despicable. From the extreme of aggressive white supremacy and white nationalism to neo-anarchic revolt against anything remotely capitalistic, we have to renew our commitment to the representation of our whole nation as well as its many diverse groups and parts. The use of *Agape* is essential to our general understanding to study and debate solutions in the particular condition we now find ourselves. The condition usually comes to us in the form of a paradox. It is everyone's fault and no one's fault at the same time. Let's take a last-ditch and reductive example of such a paradox in which it is both everyone's fault and no one's fault.

We are on a New York City subway car on our way home from wherever we came. Next to the far door stands a poor man with a shopping buggy that carries crushed cans. He is drunk with liquor. And even though he tries to keep all of the cans within his buggy, he continues to have problems keeping his cans from slipping over its sides. Every time a can drops to the floor of the subway car, he points his arm to the sky and calls out for help from someone celestial force. But he is drunk, and no one can help him in his present

133

situation. He is poor, drunk, disheveled, and crying out for spiritual guidance in a crowded subway car.

In this subway car, there are two children. One is a wealthy white Protestant from the Upper West Side of the City who begins to laugh at this tremendously funny scene. The other child next to her is a young Black-American boy who understands the plight of the poor so well, that he can only break down in tears and demand divine and social intervention and justice for this suffering poor drunk. Both children then look at each other and notice each other's reaction. They are both angry that the other reacts in such a manner to this man who can't seem to control his own world.

The young wealthy girl looks upon the Black-American boy with scorn, because this young man, given his reaction, is ruining her day. He is interfering with her right to be happy. He is interfering with her right to be happy, as she has the freedom to pursue her own happiness. Her reaction is the best reaction, because it makes her happy, as all people must be happy in order to live. His reaction is wrong, because he brings sadness and despair to her world.

The Black-American boy only knows too well what it's like for someone like the drunk man. He looks at the wealthy young woman and declares that people exactly like her are cruel and evil to the core. Never will this girl identify with the suffering of others. She will go through her life of privilege that she never earned on her own and laugh as an innocent man suffers. Even though she finds it funny, she has no right to make fun of such a tragic display of another's suffering. She does nothing at all to help this man. She can only laugh and spread her brand of cruelty throughout the country and around the world.

At this point, we must ask, knowing this condition that we are now in as observers - which child has the more appropriate response? In our system, there can only be one right and one wrong child, especially for a person who has to make a judgement. And so, there is an adult who sees all of this on the subway and is stuck with making a decision. Which child should he pick? Which child should he judge favorably? He must exit the train soon as his stop has arrived, and as the onlookers watch this unfold, the adult must come make a judgement. What will his judgement be? Which child will he select as the better child?

There answer to this is that there is no answer to this. Both children are right and both children are wrong. The adult, as he exits the train, is unsatisfied when leaving the subway car, because he realizes just then that his judgement will also be both right and wrong. What we have here is the paradox of the binary system that currently governs our democracy at this time. There is an answer but there is no answer, and even this example is a good example and a terrible example. This is how we've evolved, and this is what it has come to.

If we had the luxury of time, perhaps we may work hard to find a good escape from this paradox as many great political minds have tried to do before. And, as usual, there will be many solutions that work and many solutions that don't. But to say that there must be a finality to any kind of solution would be a strange assumption to make, especially at this point in our nation's history. Nevertheless, if every decision that must be made by our most gifted political leaders are so certain and irreversible as not to consider their own uncertainty as decision-makers within the realm of government and public service, then we can't possibly find any solution to anything at any time at all.

Most of us decide, because we must decide. If we are not using at least some kind of conception of love in our decision making, our uncertainty or our limitations will tend to vanish from our capacity to make important decisions free of the illusion of certainty. In other words, without having prior knowledge of *agape*, the adult on that subway car will always make the wrong decision, because he may not able to trust the powers of his uncertainty fully enough to throw his hands up and admit that he cannot decide at all, even though the passengers on the train label him as an incompetent or an ineffective decision-maker. He is a poor choice to guide them, because he must abstain and leave the subway car just when he is needed most.

At certain points in our humble lives, we are unable to make any decisions at all. In other words, in light of our political paradoxes that have been riddling our country, before any conflict of any kind begins, we can't really determine what decisions are right and what decisions are wrong. Should we vote for the Democrats, or should we vote for the Republicans? Should the Black-American child who understands tragedy and the fundamental need to help a down and out drunk win the ballot, or should the wealthy white child, who is laughing and loving life and wants everyone else to love life, win the ballot, because she at least understands the value of her own individual happiness and is free to pursue it in her own, unique way? They will both defend their views for the betterment of others. Yet the only real certainty we have is the certainty of the existence of the question mark.

Because there is no answer at all, we can at least begin to use *Agape* to determine what these uncertainties are and apply them to our study of political science, public choice, and political theory, even if we may not find answers right away. Whether or not we use knowledge, empathy, and faith at different times or all at once, it is better to make an effort within the creation of our most gifted and accurate political theories by making an effort. In a way, we can say that certainty will never last, while uncertainty will always last, and this uncertainty needs to apply to our vitriolic debates and arguments and all-too-vigorous attempts to find ways out of our present condition and come to a decision as to who to elect within the short time we have left before November of 2020. It is much better to use *Agape*, in other words, within our decision-making than not to use it at all. And so political science theory must also use *Agape* to understand its own government, how it ought to function, and how it leads and represents the governed.

Conclusion

There have been many who have sacrificed their lives for the ideas of love, even though they may or may not exist as we conceive of it. We can easily recall Gandhi and Dr. King and, in particular, the many who sacrificed their lives along with them, but they are no longer with us. We can remember them despite whatever they preached or whatever they achieved. Gandhi and King both shared what is common in the best of us as citizens and that is our humanity, despite whether we are fiercely individual, as capitalism demands, or stubbornly collective, as a socialist society demands.

Sir Winston Churchill can even be of greater interest to us. He is of much interest, because his attitudes and beliefs closely mirror the type of extremism that is occurring now. Domestically and internationally, Churchill was a solid conservative, and during his rise into greater government life, the people of Britain were mostly liberal. It was nearly the same as it was when Hillary Rodham Clinton lost the election to Donald J. Trump.

Mostly seen as a brash, land-holding royalist and an ultra-conservative in the British Parliament, the Admiral of the British Navy, Churchill, when he first proposed war with Hitler's Germany, was seen by most in Britain as an overbearing, unfeeling, greedy, and grossly obese 'warmonger,' as many had called him way back when. He was even quoted publicly in the 1930s as saying something very negative about his arch-rival at the time, Mahatma Gandhi, who had been gaining incredible popularity in Britain. Churchill said,

> "It is alarming and also nauseating to see
> Mr. Gandhi, a seditious Middle Temple lawyer
> of the type well-known in the East, now posing
> as a fakir, striding half naked up the steps of the
> Vice-Regal Palace to parley on equal terms
> with the representative of the King-Emperor."

A *fakir*, as best described in many encyclopedia and dictionaries, is a Muslim Sufi holy man or woman who lives on only what he or she gets by begging. A *fakir* is a wandering Middle Eastern or South Asian monk who follows the Islamic faith, or Sufism, which is a mystical branch of Islam. There are also *fakirs* in Hinduism as well.

In his journals detailing the prelude to the Second World War, Churchill, however, admitted how the many comments made against him, especially the 'warmonger' statements that the masses hurled at him before the war's painful start, wounded him personally and hurt his feelings, the reactions and his attacks towards Gandhi notwithstanding. Similarly, he felt that millions upon millions of lives would have to be sacrificed to fight the Second World War as well. He was deeply saddened and depressed about this too. And yet this incredibly flawed human being with many, many faults, and dealing with untreated bi-polar disorder is said to have single-handedly, and through the Herculean efforts of the countless many more who died and were injured saved Western Civilization and the rest of the world, for that matter, from the clutches of European fascism.

Jesus was at first a simple Jewish Carpenter. As St. Augustine brilliantly argues, Jesus had to progress, or what we would now say, evolve, from a single, simple human being into The Father, The Son, and The Holy Ghost - the Paradox of Three and One, sorted out through patience and time, of all things, by the careful deliberation of a humble Christian monk.

Muhammad had to conquer Medina and Mecca as a warrior to free Arabia from Paganism and even married a woman much older to add knowledge and wisdom to his growing position. And yet he gave Arabia a God that finally made sense to a warring people.

Moses served in the Egyptian army as a successful General and a Master Builder and soon became the right-hand trustee of the Great Pharaoh's succession. He then went on to free the Hebrews from bondage and all of the atrocities of Egyptian slavery to the detriment of the same Egyptian ruling family who loved him and raised him from the day they had adopted him. He felt this pain too.

Despite Einstein's incredible genius, in middle school he was a below average student in Mathematics. Yet his steadfast devotion to pacifist principles and his eventual genius in physics and mathematics inadvertently and unwittingly contributed to one of the worst humanitarian disasters in all of human history. A very simple military and political mindset outsmarted him. It broke him by the end of his life, and, of course, we never hear about the inevitable self-destruction of this great man.

All of these men, and also the many women involved in their lives, all had to be human beings first before being anything remotely great. Joan of Arc had to fight as a fierce warrior of France despite her nervousness and misgivings of fighting. Even the devoted Mother Theresa, in all of her selfless desires to help even the sickest and most unwanted children in all of the world, admitted towards the end of her life that she had to battle, quite troublingly, with the darkness and doubts of her own riddled thoughts.

These weren't perfect people. They had flaws, just as the Greek and Roman Gods had their flaws of having inherent human qualities, manipulating their subjects, and squabbling amongst themselves. But what is true of them all is that, despite their flaws and their apparent imperfections, they all supported this notion of love in any collective society and among all individuals.

It is vitally important at this time to get back to love's important fundamentals so that the future citizens who will soon inherit this country and also this Earth do not merely have to survive or painfully exist in the Hell that we have all equally created as a free and equal peoples, but so they have the opportunity to live as well, despite the flaws of their ancestors who may face the danger of now living much longer than their children ever will. We are all at fault and we are all to blame in many ways, but perhaps through the implementation of love's principles, we are never too late.

Other Issues and Problems (Appendix)

The Media

Ever since the inception of new technologies, like the telegraph and then the radio, the media has always been a consistent force on the stage of the American political landscape. Ever since Edward R. Morrow of *CBS News* first investigated Senator Joseph McCarthy's *Red Scare*, the news of print journalism, radio, and the omnipresence of nonfiction books have usually taken an adversarial role towards government, whether that government is headed by the Democrats or the Republicans.

When the first televised debates between then Senator John F. Kennedy and Vice President Richard M. Nixon appeared magically on the television sets in many homes across the nation, it became apparent how television would soon become a dominating force in American government and soon thereafter "The Fourth Estate of Government".

When Walter Cronkite anchored *The CBS Evening News* during the Kennedy assassination in the early 1960s, many watched in horror as he reported Kennedy's murder, removed his glasses from the bridge of his nose, and rubbed his eyes in exhaustion and dismay. At the time, Walter Cronkite was then regarded as the most trusted man in

America, and to have him openly express his emotions in front of the nation sent chills up and down many an American's arms at the time.

This dramatically changed, however, when television news began to change with the rise of three dominant network television and radio stations and also the beginning of The Public Broadcasting System. There was now fierce competition for news on television, while the print media soon followed suit. Nevertheless, there was a happy blend of radio, print, and television news. All of them still maintained their adversarial stance towards government. As far as print news was concerned, *The New York Times* grew in reputation to become the paper of record, and *The Washington Post* comprehensively reported the goings-on and crucial events of all three branches of government.

But when the Civil Rights Movement began to take shape as well as alternative forms of art and writings by the Beat Generation and the 1960s Counter-Culture, for example, the media took on a very different form from that of the past. Add to these the student protests that rippled across many college and university campuses in the mid-1960s, and suddenly a once moderate and civil conservative and liberal discourse among those in the media had split even wider apart.

For the most part, especially in the few years just before President Kennedy had committed troops to Vietnam to hedge against the Communist threat and support the ebbing power of colonial France in South Asia, the pendulum began to shift once more. Many would argue that it was the Kennedy assassination that began this shift, especially when then Vice-President Lyndon B. Johnson suddenly filled his role as President of the nation, albeit reluctantly. But under the Johnson administration, the Conflict in Vietnam continued to escalate. And so many of the younger journalists who pledged their allegiance against the escalation of this conflict swung far to the left in their points of view and began to write articles that reflected the growing concerns of what most of their generation thought about the Vietnam Conflict, not to mention the violent murder of Dr. Martin Luther King, Jr. just after President Kennedy's assassination.

This incredible shift in journalistic ideology had to be dealt with by the concerns of many newspaper editors, as many of their young, talented journalists were evading their more fundamental journalistic principles to take part in a growing Anti-War movement that soon threw a powder-keg through the Main Streets of society. These newspapers and television broadcasts vividly portrayed this awkward and new society that began to question government power in a land that many had thought had represented the good of the people and held the public trust. But what occurred at *The New York Times* during this time was extraordinary for the media. When managing editor A.M. Rosenthal directed his journalists into the new territory known as 'objectivity' in news reporting, things began to change dramatically.

Rosenthal himself was personally conservative and had worked with his journalists and developed the news stories in a more traditional vein that kept journalism more traditional and yet still adversarial. But as the Conflict in Vietnam progressed, when the Nixon Administration came to power, and as the revelation of the Pentagon Papers exposed more of the details of government overreach and corruption, Rosenthal noticed that his journalists, especially the younger reporters, were turning increasingly radical in their views and in their reporting.

Young editors began selecting news that featured protests against the Vietnam War than the goings-on of government. More weight was given to the youth of the country and their Counter-Cultural movement more than ever before, culminating in President Richard M. Nixon's resignation as leader of the free world.

Even though Rosenthal was personally conservative in most ways, he dictatorially imposed a policy to have all of his reporters, no matter their political prejudices or opinions, age or experience, report all of their news 'objectively.' And this basically meant that news had to be reported in an unbiased, unprejudiced, and impartial manner that took into account both sides of a story, or even in many cases, all sides of a story. This gave the reader a broader picture of the many points of view that a single issue or event could take. This was a remarkable feat, because now both, if not all, sides of a conventional news story would no longer include the political biases of the reporters themselves but include both, if not all, sides of an issue.

But even though Rosenthal enforced this policy at *The Times*, the paper was still thought of as a liberal paper as a result of their narrative style of reporting compared to a newspaper like that of *The Wall Street Journal* that reported sparse, to-the-point information in a tight format, was viewed by most as more conservative. Even though objectivity had a huge impact on journalism at the time, the newspapers themselves were still viewed by many as politically different but not by such a wide margin. For its time, objectivity worked.

Increasingly, however, many critics of the media argued that objectivity was increasingly impossible to implement. Many argued that the idea of objectivity in news was a complete myth and even though editors like Rosenthal had tried to maintain their reporting to with an even-hand and a balanced approach, it was obvious to many that biases still came through. The problem, however, may not have been with the idea of objectivity itself but the *ideal* of objectivity and how it may have been too far a reach for most of the news media. What continued to exacerbate this criticism was the continued staffing of those same young reporters who still clung to the old vestiges of the Civil Rights Movement and the Anti-Vietnam Protests. This continued after the Ford Administration and then followed President Carter into the neo-conservative Reagan presidency.

But when the country had to shift focus, the staffing within the media was such that many of the young reporters, who were decidedly politically liberal, and as the conservative old guard had silently faded into the background, the ideology of the Reagan Administration wasn't properly represented in the news. Many neo-conservatives who pledged their alliance to the resurrection of traditional conservative values and the pressing need for economic prosperity were looked over or even ignored by some newspapers in favor of more liberal and more experienced leaders of a prior generation. The ones in charge of the media, then, were those who inherited the legacy of the assassination of President Kennedy, a stubborn and never-ending Cold War, and of course, a renewed adversarialism towards the new leadership of the Reagan Administration that had begun to change the country entirely.

Within all areas of media, conservative reporting had been resurrected with a new generation of conservative thinkers and a new selection of news items that reflected conservative ideas. Yet it seemed as though many liberals didn't want to change with the times no matter what sacrifices had been made. It was here that the media soon began to change form.

Bill Engberg, after the horrific attacks of September 11th, was one of the first veteran reporters to come out of his shell about the consistent liberal bias in the media. Back then, Mr. Engberg worked as a television reporter for the venerable *CBS News* which had been the subject of increasing criticism by a growing conservative public. At the time, Anchor Dan Rather, a veteran news reporter as well as a particularly dedicated and highly-regarded newsman who first covered the Kennedy assassination as a television reporter in Houston, steered the ship of *CBS News* as its Managing Editor as well as Anchor.

Yet most of the country colored Mr. Rather as a fierce liberal at a time of shifting American values. Whether or not this criticism of him was valid is questionable, because many of his supporters saw him as dedicated to more timeless journalistic principles than anything else and not any sort of political opinion-maker that kept his newsroom on the liberal side. Nevertheless, reporters like Engberg began revealing that most news organizations were no longer reporting the news fairly due to liberal biases that had institutionalized the media as a "liberal" industry. Readers and viewers alike were getting skewed reporting and hardly anyone had taken notice, because it had gone on for so long. The stage was then set for a Juggernaut of conservative news like the country had never seen before. Even the great William F. Buckley, Jr. had never witnessed anything like it before. Enter Rupert Murdoch's *Fox News*.

If we fast-forward to our world of today, as of this writing we now have twenty-four-hour, round-the-clock news. What started out as Ted Turner's intrepid *CNN Headline News* experiment and his continuation of the traditional news format, objectivity still remained in the news for as long as it could. But with a continuation of *CNN* as the premier source of 24/7 news, talk-shows, documentaries, and other news programming that reflected traditional news were added into the blend.

CNN's *Crossfire*, for example, featured contemporary news stories that two commentators debated one-on-one. These two commentators were both liberal on one side, and conservative on the other. But rarely was there a moment when the two commentators ever argued ferociously.

Actually, their opinions were explained rationally, cogently, and in a way that most people who watched the program could easily understand. The two commentators even shared laughter and occasional chuckles, and were probably, at the end of their tenure, very good friends and held each other in high esteem. But never was there the slightest bit of competitiveness, vitriol, or even a raised voice between the two. It was comfortable to watch, and after the program, they returned to their writing desks and wrote articles for the magazines they worked for. One could say the same of the liberal attorney Ron Kuby and Guardian Angel's founder Curtis Sliwa, as they debated issues of criminal justice on ABC Talk-Radio in New York City. Once media communities like these openly declared that most media outlets were biased, however, especially just following the September 11th attacks, a completely different media took shape, and the country was forever changed through the information it received.

The emergence of three dominant, 24/7 news channels emerged. These were *CNN*, *Fox*, and *MSNBC*, most of them developed during the dramatic economic expansion and the rise of the Internet at the height of the popularity of the Clinton Administration. From this, the information age continued and the digital age was born. New technology revolutionized newsrooms, and so these three 24/7 news channels, as well as other news networks in general, gained more ground and gained even more dominance in delivering news to its viewers. It even crippled the newspaper industry and print as an entire medium.

The print industry, however, continues to gain ground, especially online, but local and regional print newspapers were hit the hardest and faded fast. The whole nation had to rely on the corporate news channels to retrieve their information by personalities and other news sources. Whatever independent news organizations were left over had to close up shop, and this also included the grassroots, well-regarded newspapers and magazines that weren't backed by large corporations. And the large, multi-national media conglomerates continued to add the smaller, more vulnerable media news outlets to their ever-expanding asset portfolios.

But these three 24/7 news channels, which commanded the country's focus, began to diverge from one another as the competition among these networks escalated. Fairly quickly, *CNN* was seen easily by many as left of center. *MSNBC* was seen as left of center but also more liberal and entertaining. And then there was *Fox News*, the truly all-conservative media news channel. It's brand of reporting did include some counter-point liberals to balance some of its news programs, but this didn't last for very long, especially just after the bombing of the World Trade Center in New York

City. It was then, during the years of the Bush Administration and the coming years of the wars in the Middle East that these three networks diverged, and they diverged rapidly and with a celerity that struck many as even dangerous to the fabric of the nation and how the public received its news.

All three of these networks, highly competitive and ratings-mad, grew bolder in their opinions, and fairly soon, even liberal and conservative counterpoints were eliminated from their broadcasts until we have the news of today, where we have news selection that completely pulls to one political side or the other, where each talk show host insults the other from their own separate on-screen pulpits, and slowly, each major news outlet, be that print, television, or online website, increasingly reflects the political opinions of their owners, and what is of most concern here, the cleavage between each of the two dominating political parties. Most now understand and acknowledge that objectivity in the news has died ever since the September 11th attacks. What started as an admission of bias in casual news opinions and debates has created a public that is now split on either side of the enormous political divide that we are left with today.

What may help, however, if it is still not too late, is to return to the balanced, traditional reporting that was lost so long ago. A.M. Rosenthal's objectivity is, quite arguably, the best approach we may have to bring this tremendous national divide together. A simple admission of media bias and the bandwagon rush to declare that objectivity had been a myth to begin with and to criticize it as a relic of the past will have to be reversed in order to bring stability and more harmony to a public that is at each other's throats. While this doesn't necessarily have to happen in cyberspace or for any specific news channel, there still has to be a choice, no matter how small or low-funded, that delivers objective news reporting to the public. Even a small television news program like this would at least be a start and would offer a news alternative to those disaffected centrists who have given up on any future stability for the nation. Because what remains now can easily be seen as a serious national security risk that threatens to split the current chasm between the two political sides even wider into the chaos of physical warfare and violence, not to mention a conflict between two regions of the country, the South and the Midwest, and the Eastern/Western areas of the country. We have plenty of examples of this already, and we needn't say more about it. We should at least try, at least try to revisit A.M. Rosenthal's work, and learn about his contributions to this ideal known as objectivity. Bill Engberg, if we ask him today, might even agree with us.

Generational Differences

The differences among generations is also a cause of grave concern. In the past, generations have always had their differences, mainly between old and young. But lately, (and while this is still the same historically), other generational factors have to be taken into consideration to avoid many a turbulent election period.

The generational gap in attitudes and thinking have grown considerably wider over the years, but it is very important to note, however, that it would be false to pigeon-hole or stereotype all members of a certain generation as having same general characteristics. We can, however, safely assume through media reports some anecdotal evidence, and the information that we already have within our own families that there does exist a few general characteristics of each predominant generation, even though the individuals within these generations may differ among each other widely.

It is also important to note that individuals within generations who consider themselves culturally different or apart from the mainstream perception of the characteristics may not be adequately known enough to write about accurately. Again, all of the information and knowledge that we have about each predominant generation is only a recounting of general, if not totally vague, characteristics or stereotypes, and as we begin to discuss them here, we should be well aware that it is usually impossible to group any single generation as being defined in ay way apart from another, regardless of how specific these characterizations may seem. But we will try here, just to show the great generational divides that exist within our nation at this time, mostly as a result of the great divide and polarization that currently exists between the extreme conservative public and extreme liberal public.

We will first start with the oldest generation in our nation, or those that are now of old age or those who came of age during the Second Word War. Ever since the bombing of Pearl Harbor by the Japanese and the entrance of the United States into this astounding war, mostly as a result of Winston Churchill's need to protect Europe from the growing tide of fascism in Italy and Germany as well as an oil embargo to the island country of Japan, along with other factors, such as arms support from the US to Great Britain, the generation that fought this war is considered to be the "greatest" one, as journalist Tom Brokaw of *NBC News* had termed the phrase.

Millions perished during the war, and American democracy was saved, despite a terrible nuclear attack on Japan which was mainly due to the pure exhaustion of the war by the American people. Many of the World War Two generation have been praised by political conservatives for serving their country and their country's interests in the best way possible. This generation generally espouses more 'old-fashioned' values, such as strong marriages and families, a veneration for American traditions and history, and a rigorous work ethic to achieve 'The American Dream'. Many of this generation are proud of how they served their country selflessly and returned from the war and built a good, strong, and stable economy that benefited the generations that followed. And while many of them did grow out of the Great Depression and had humble values and simpler lives, it was the generations that came after them that this greatest generation of all was also held responsible for many of the systemic social problems that gave impetus to the Civil Rights Movement and other such movements.

It is also important to note here that this generation was also faulted for unjustly imprisoning Japanese-American citizens in internment camps, even though they were ensured the full rights and protections guaranteed by the Constitution as U.S. citizens. Many younger generals would even go so far as to say that such a generation, no matter what they sacrificed and at what cost, were ignorant in how they followed their government blindly into a war that nearly destroyed the nation itself. Many critics would argue that the nation did not have to get involved in such a war, since it was not a fundamental part of Europe anyway. Similarly, our greatest generation looks upon the generation that followed it with a particular disdain for its lack of patriotism, its lack of values, as well as its loose morality, and evasion of faith and religion. The great divide, then, especially during the heightening crisis in Vietnam had already existed between this greatest of generations and whom we can now safely call, 'The Baby Boomers'.

Interestingly enough, the Baby Boomers are a generation of people that got its name from the skyrocketing birthrate that occurred just after the Pearl Harbor attacks. It was a growing trend to have young families procreate in case husbands who had to fight overseas never returned from battle. It was a scary time, and the fear that these men would never return gave reason for families to procreate in case these men never returned.

Also, many women who stayed behind filled many male roles in industry and government until they were asked to leave when their husbands returned from the war. It is also widely known that during this period, there were very few opponents of the war, very few pacifists, and very few resistors. Due to the attack on Pearl Harbor, most of the public agreed that the country had a moral imperative to defend itself and rid the world of an imperial enemy.

159

Interestingly enough, Baby Boomers are the children of these parents who fought in World War Two. Baby Boomers were born in the 1950s, and when their fathers returned from war, if they ever returned, they were the beneficiaries of an enormous prosperity as a result of the Allied victory over the near-undefeatable fascist forces of Europe and Japan.

Many of these children, who had grown up humbly, entered the middle classes as well as the upper-middle class of a growing and prosperous America. But Russia had taken a huge hit as a result of the war, as many more there had died compared to those soldiers of the U.S. and British soldiers. Once the war was over, the Soviet Union, headed dictatorially by Joseph Stalin, looked upon the West with great suspicion, as though the Soviet Union had been cheated by them at the end of the war. The Russians also eyed the prosperity gained by America and Great Britain as well as its expansion of power and influence over the world as threatening to the interests of the Soviet Union and Communism in general. Thus, even though the Allies had won the war and many benefits were had by all winning sides, the Baby Boomers, despite a vague promise that the Second War would be the last war ever to grace the face of the Earth, suddenly confronted the reality of the Cold War and nuclear annihilation.

But it didn't end there. As a direct result of the Cold War, they faced the daunting task of the Korean War as a direct result of the American attempt to curtain Soviet influence in Asia. And finally, the Baby Boomers faced the ultimate test of being drafted in an ongoing fight against Communism in Vietnam.

Many were young and coming of age during the escalation of this conflict. Many of this generation witnessed friends, loved ones, and the people they once knew in high school returning in body bags as the death toll steadily rose. But it wasn't exactly fear that thrusted the Baby Boomers to side against the Vietnam War. They also inherited the Kennedy Assassination, Black Nationalism, and the assassination of Martin Luther King, Jr. Arguably, this particular generation faced an uncertain future. They had been caught in the middle of turbulent social movements and encouraged to fight against the oppression of their elders by professors within their colleges and universities who were against the war. Even some teachers in High School discouraged their students from enlisting. And what started as a few isolated protests at only a handful of universities and small colleges turned into an Anti-War Movement so powerful that it amounted to an all-out revolution against the government, and in many cases against their own families, who were dismayed and disillusioned that their sons and

161

daughters wouldn't enter the frays of battle for them as they had done for them in World War Two and Korea.

After this outright rebellion, as well as Nixon's landslide election after Johnson's term came to an end, a tradition of rebellion still remained. Many have argued that it was this new trend of rebellion as well as Nixon's continued bombing of Vietnam to achieve any kind of victory there and bring the unpopular war to a quick but brutal end, that Nixon was stripped of his office and was forced to resign. Many would argue that Vietnam was the real reason behind Nixon's oust from office and not Watergate. Whether or not this is true is debatable, but many still see it that way. The resignation of Nixon was really the nation's referendum on the tragic consequences of entering the Vietnam Conflict.

But the Baby Boomers still had to continue, and despite many advances in the areas of social justice, government ethics reform, and the handling of issues of race and sex, such as the rise of the Feminist movement and the Gay Rights movement, many Baby Boomers lacked capital and needed it to withstand a tanking economy and a general lack of prosperity after Carter took office soon after Ford's vacated the presidency. Many of these Baby Boomers couldn't go home after the war, as the split between the Greatest Generation and these Baby Boomers was both wide and fierce.

When Ronald Reagan was elected, the country finally saw growth, and many of these 'hippies' and 'yippies' of the past discarded their tie-dies, head-bands, ripped jeans, and protest banners, and soon prospered as 'yuppies.' A new breed of conservative under President Reagan soon prospered. And so, the growing divide within the Baby Boom generation itself grew, because many saw Reagan's domestic policies as ending a horrible period of ever-present poverty, crime, and lack of adequate protection by police, especially in densely populated urban areas. But it is interesting to note here, that all Baby Boomers didn't play along. Many of them still held fast to the memories of what had been gained during the 1960s and held on to an era that refused to vanish so quickly, even though these neo-conservatives hoped to end the legacy of Vietnam for themselves rather than continue struggling. They wanted to leave it behind, while the other half wanted it to evolve and grow.

After President George H.W. Bush's single-term in office, and the hard work of his administration of guiding the post-Reagan economy out of what it wanted most: incredible prosperity, social justice, dramatic cutbacks in military and defense funding, and an overall harmonious sense of well-being combined with a continuation of older Anti-War and Civil Rights ideology. With Reagan, Bush, and Clinton, this once embattled Baby Boomer generation suddenly prospered together like never before. The Soviet Union had fallen under Reagan. War was out of the picture, and what was once a difficult climb from out of the Carter presidency, now settled into a prosperous retirement. But what about their children?

A novel by Canadian author Douglas Coupland coined the term "Generation X". This name was quickly used by the mainstream media to describe the generation that grew up during the Reagan Era. Interestingly enough, Generation X is a transitional generation that is mainly seen as the bridge between Reagan's conservative revival of prosperity and the kind of 1960s Counter-Cultural reverence that was a product of prior trends in art, music, fashion, and politics.

Reagan did neglect the AIDS Crisis, and many Black-Americans felt excluded from his promises to rebuild urban centers after the waves of crime and poverty that swept through such as areas as New York, Detroit, and Los Angeles. Crime held cities hostage during the late 1970s and early 1980s. But a newer breed was born that bridged the gap between 1950s tradition and 1960s idealism and rebellion.

Generation X, if we are permitted to define them as that, was the beneficiary of their parent's wealth, due to investments that boomed during Reagan. But this all changed when the stock market soon crashed at its height and sent markets plummeting as many lost all of their money on junk bonds and overvalued stocks. Once this happened, the prosperity of the Reagan years was brought to an end. President George H.W. Bush cleaned up the mess, only to lose to Bill Clinton after only a single term. But only after three or four years of recession, the Clinton Administration also delivered in a big way on the economy, thus providing Generation X'ers with even more wealth and more opportunity than ever before. The Generation X'ers were the immediate beneficiaries of both Reagan and Clinton. We can say, then, that Generation X, as well as the generation that soon followed it, Generation Y, soon became two of the most fortunate generations ever to grace the pages of American History.

Issues for Millennials to Consider

When September 11th came to pass, the nation geared up for another war, and so those in high school at the time, the ones who grew up under Bill Clinton and were promised the world, faced the Internet bubble, an immediate lack of jobs, and an older economy that relied chiefly on energy commodities, like oil and coal, that they really didn't have any familiarity with. The only real option for this Millennial generation, who came of age at the beginning of the George W. Bush years, was the prospect of going to war in Iraq and Afghanistan as being in the Armed Services became the only way out of joblessness and poverty. Military funding was immediately and dramatically restored to finance the war in the Middle East and included benefits that not many youths could turn down. And many did enlist in the Military, but the others who remained behind either faced unemployment, drug addiction, huge college loan debts (if they could afford the cost of a college education at all) and a lack of adequate health insurance.

This continued through the Obama Administration, which did bring much needed relief to the nation, but President Bush left office with the economy in shambles, as a banking crisis and predatory loan and mortgage practices nearly crippled the nation. Many believed that the nation was heading into a depression only to be brought back to life by the Obama Administration with the approval of Congress.

While the Bush Administration stressed the importance of unregulated capitalism, the Obama Administration understood that the country could tank economically. Financial firms that were "too big to fail" found many Millennials disillusioned by a nation that refused to wean itself off the bad practices of those who were already wealthy. Also, much of the culture focused on the needs of the generation just prior to them instead of addressing the Millennial's concerns. It is no surprise, then, that this Millennial generation has a right to be angry and upset with a nation that has totally neglected its interests.

After the stock bubble crash during the Clinton Administration, this suffering generation was ignored and pushed into a war that they didn't want, unless, of course, these young people believed so strongly in the aims of Bush's War that they quickly enlisted without knowing what they had signed up for. Eighteen years later, this war is supposed to end because of the promise made by President Trump to quickly withdraw troops from Afghanistan and Syria. The forces in Iraq would remain there and dare we say democratize or even colonize the country. While most Millennials are relieved by this proposed pullout, there is no question that many of them resent the wealthy and the success of their predecessors as well as the gains in technology made under Clinton.

The Millennials witnessed the gap between rich and poor widening, and many of them remained poor, while the older generations grew wealthy and were provided access to government services that ensured some degree of comfort. And yet the Trump Administration, while lowering unemployment to manageable levels, only maintained the part-time service economy where Millennials faced a future of part-time jobs for very low wages. Trump refused to raise the minimum wage, until Congress and state governments forced corporations and businesses to do so. This rise in wages, however, will still take several years to go into effect. Also, many Millennials even have to work two, sometimes three jobs to survive. Many have turned to addiction. Many have dropped out of college, as they can no longer afford it. And we can argue here that Millennials are also a generation that is now of great threat to older generations who have prospered under much more favorable political and economic circumstances.

For the Millennial generation, there is plenty to be concerned about, both in terms of the dangers they pose to their society and the world, as well as the threats they face to their own generation as well. But what is perhaps even more striking, the danger the Millennial generation poses to others is real and will most likely pose to the 2020 election period, now that it is almost here. Because along with their staggering disenfranchisement comes their need to react to a country and government system that has neglected their interests.

In what is expected to be one of the most volatile election periods in decades, the Millennial generation seems no longer interested in non-violent forms of social protest as their Baby Boomer predecessors. Rather, as we can see in places like New York City during the *Republican National Convention* of President George W. Bush's re-election campaign and recently in Seattle's violent street protests there just prior to President Trump's election, and the violent exchanges between White Supremacists in Charlottesville and Portland (and those who oppose them), and the many mass shootings in El Paso, Dayton, and Gilroy, and impending environmental catastrophes may signal to the entire nation that there is a significant enough security threat to merit at least some concern about what our next election period may bring. Millennials will take center stage in those protests then. In other words, most Millennials, whether they are justified or not, no longer see non-violent forms of social protest as effective in bringing about social change or addressing issues of social justice. Actually, if we look at the recent trends in our country since Trump took office, these suggest that Millennials will justify using violence to achieve what they want.

Certainly, this is troubling news, especially for older generations who are living longer and more prosperous lives as a result of the nation's past desire for economic prosperity and also the desire to maintain American exceptionalism to sustain or even augment that prosperity. But Millennials also need to understand some things before this election period that they should always keep in mind.

We will explain them here, but before we begin any discussion about Millennials, it is important to note that in no means is the following explanation an attempt at some vague form of didacticism. This would simply be insulting to a generation that has studied the past closely and has still found it wanting, to say the least. They have learned enough and are suffering enough to take anything learned from their elders with a grain of salt. But it is an attempt to explain, in simple terms, what needs to be known about the past in order for them more than they are already informed. It is neither an attempt to present arguments that justify the past, nor is it an attempt to inform them. They already know. It is simply a review of ideas that Millennials must consider before any violent action on their part takes place during this upcoming election period.

Just to clarify who these Millennials are, the Pew Research Center defines them as anyone who is currently between the ages of 24 and 38, born between 1981 and 1994. Already, we can sense trouble. We remember the rioting that took place at Woodstock II as a prime example of the angst of such a generation, and yes, it has gotten even worse. Even though Millennials may be perfectly justified in their anger, there are severe consequences for using violence as a form of social protest, even though it does indeed garner the most media coverage, even more so than older, more tired forms of non-violent social protest.

Such violence may indeed take center stage or capture the headlines of *The New York Times* and be featured on every media channel imaginable, but historically speaking, while government often winces at mass non-violent protests because they cannot do much to respond to them, much of the country, especially those in seats of power, will urge swift action to protect, not only families, but also important business interests when violent protests take place. Law enforcement will do the same, not only because of local and state economic interests, but simply for the protection of the innocent. This is what the police take a personal interest in. Even during tumultuous periods of non-violent protest, the police who used violence were universally shunned by most in the country and were painted as immoral, unjustified, and corrupt. So, when we assume that the police cannot do much to quell non-violent protests, we are most likely accurate in the assumption that they will do everything they can to quell protests that are violent.

Most of the country will be justified in using the police to crush violent protest, no matter the issue. It will be covered by mass media. It will be discussed. It will be debated. But mostly, it will be suppressed and extinguished by the use of a counter-violence that will be deemed justified by most of the country. This is just a fact of life in most, if not all, countries, no matter how disagreeable this may seem to the Millennial generation.

Similarly, there have been arguments made against violent forms of social protests by past leaders, mostly by pacifists. Whether or not non-violence is both feasible or reliable within Western democracies anymore is debatable at this time. We cannot discount the practical arguments of Gandhi who boldly declared that a few British soldiers cannot control the whole population of India, much to the disappointment and consternation of many of his supporters who wanted to use violence against the British. Nor can we discount the even more vital arguments against the rising tide of Black Nationalism when Dr. King argued that a few black revolutionaries will never overthrow a majority of white citizens. Even the more recent conflict in Charlottesville, where a small group of non-violent participants and observers actually sang spiritual songs to soothe the violent intentions of white nationalists who were struck by a paralysis of sorts and wide stares in shock and awe, as Dr. Cornell West vividly described it, has not been seen by Millennials as particularly effective at all.

For Millennials who are considering using violence, neo-anarchists in particular, we must also remember that, even though the Anti-Vietnam protests did usher in long-lasting social changes, it never changed the fact that George McGovern only won one state while Richard M. Nixon won all the others. Even though Nixon wanted to bring a quick end to the War in Vietnam, it also accelerated the mass killing of thousands of innocent Vietnamese. In other words, most citizens, both young and old, even though they may sympathize with the current plight of the Millennial generation, would also be more than willing to crush any form of violent protest before it could spiral out of control. Law enforcement will first isolate it, contain it, and then extinguish it. This is just a basic fact of life.

Similarly, innocent people may be harmed or even killed by any violent Millennial protest, which provides even more justification for law enforcement to injure or maim violent protesters to protect the innocent. This should provide even more reason for those considering rioting as a form of social protest to question whether or not rioting is the best response to injustice. This is not an attempt to frighten or thwart any form of protest that may occur during our upcoming elections. It is simply an attempt to state what has factually been the case in all countries, no matter the type of government in power.

Similarly, it is false to assume that the Millennial generation is somehow united and will rally around the same arguments, issues, causes, and justifications for protesting. Like the generations before them, and just like the pendulum that swings within the borders of any Western democracy, many Millennials will definitely support the Trump Administration in the upcoming elections. Even within their own generation, Millennials will encounter many forms of violent counter-protests as well. And if the Millennials are remotely successful, and if such violence becomes the norm in the regions where such protest take place, what we can count on is the slow vanishing of the businesses and institutions that aid the many in progressing within already economically challenged areas. The places where these protests take place will see the immediate effects of this. What may result is what is commonly known as a 'brain drain' as well as a flight of commerce and business that could have otherwise funded state and local governments to alleviate an entire generation of its most pressing burdens.

For instance, during the rioting that followed the assassination of Dr. King in such prosperous urban centers as Detroit, Watts, and Newark, rioting resulted in a common trend known as "white flight," even though there were many in the nation who saw the rioting as justified after Dr. King's brutal assassination. The result of this white flight was impoverished, vacant, and economically stagnant urban centers that were never able to recover, even though every effort had been made in their recovery for the several decades that followed. Yes, the scars inevitably remain. The same is true for the more recent rioting in South Central, Los Angeles during the early 1990s. Even though the Rodney King incident of police brutality captured the hearts and minds of many, and even through reforms and the eventual prosecution of the policemen involved were made, this section of Los Angeles will never fully recover for years, perhaps even decades.

There will always be negative consequences for using violence to rail against any form of injustice. Millennials must keep this in mind. And even though, this election is an important one, every election period seems to the 'the most important election in history.' Many could argue that *Bush v. Gore* was the most important election in history as well. It is not the same for every generation. And while this election may have dire consequences that go along with it, the same was true of the election of Abraham Lincoln as well. And time marches on…

Many of the Millennial generation are suddenly in a unique position and have an even greater opportunity than any generation that came before it. They still have much time to utilize the powers of the imagination and the forces of their own creativity to construct ideas about alternative systems of government that the generations of those before it never had. To borrow from what Churchill said in an example that may counter how many may view our American democracy at the present time, that "a democracy like ours is the worst of all forms of government, except for the many worse that have already been tried," is self-defeating for many Millennials who have yet to imagine what any other system of government might be like. But they must also remember that any other system other than democracy may also be much worse.

Older generations just don't have time to create again. Similarly, time will be on their side, and to use it in violent rebellion is simply a waste of this time. Millennials could instead discuss and exchange their ideas, not to older generations who would most likely reject them, but amongst themselves without resorting to bringing the whole system down. Imagining new and alternative government systems that address our binary flaws is just but one example of many constructive responses they can make instead of using violence to dismantle our current political system, no matter how dysfunctional it may be.

Peaceful forms of protest may indeed not work anymore, but nothing yet has been imagined that would work better. Millennials are in the best position to discover new ways to change government and the ways in which we protest and speak truth to power to both the men and women in extraordinary positions of power, wealth, and status, because most will soon know that the needs of the entire Millennial generation continue to be unmet by a nation that has turned a blind eye to them. Millennials also have to know that they themselves may encounter the same divide that older generations are faced with now as well one day.

Furthermore, they also have to consider issues that their own generation will undoubtedly have to confront when it is their turn to take power, just as the generations that came before them had to, not only for themselves, but or younger generations that came after them. They must deal with bullying in the schools, drug addiction, the needs of their families and the healthcare of their elders, et cetera.

They must also realize that the same mass psychology of scapegoating is used time and again, not necessarily to propel any such party or dictator to the height of power or one generation to lash out and triumph over another but to save the mass of a population from its smaller and least powerful parts. This is the hallmark of any society or any collection of individuals, whether it is scapegoating in the American work place, the traditional American family, or a strong and mighty nation at odds with itself facing widespread starvation or a terrible guilt and also reparations after losing a war.

American Muslims are but one important example of a people that may never get the attention they deserve from a nation that doesn't have any information on how many innocent people have been killed overseas yet. There are countless others who have been scapegoated in the past - the Jews in Nazi Germany (and in Christianity and Islam, in general), the Buddhists in Tibet within the territory of a much mightier China, the fleeing Rohingya Muslims of Burma who had to migrate to Bangladesh, the defenseless Christian woman who made a simple mistake in Muslim Pakistan, the Christian Armenians in Turkey, the genocides in Bangladesh, Sudan, East Timor, and the others that will inevitably follow.

Again, it is every generation's fault through no fault of their own, but what is most important here is that this scapegoating takes place all the time here in the United States as well. If we see this scapegoating, we hope it's not aimed at us. Is it the genuine fear of the loss of our nation, then, or is it the love of the many who have to be saved at the expense of the few? Millennials will have to deal with these same issues as they age.

The New Feminism (Post-Hillary Clinton)

What has become ever-increasingly violent is the new political position that many Millennial feminists now find themselves in. Many feminists, both on the ground and in the high towers of academia, are suddenly beginning to see violence as a just method for redressing heinous sexual crimes. Many contemporary radical feminists now see violence as a justified response to these sex crimes without any further reliance on the institutions of justice that have outlawed such criminal activity and behaviors.

While rape, domestic abuse, and other forms of violence towards women are always heinous and unjust, there are women who will now justify taking justice into their own hands to seek the punishment, they believe, fits the crime involved. This, no doubt, is a dangerous trend, and while violent sex crimes are definitely an example of what is worst in our society, it is important that we compare this new trend of thought to what traditional feminists once believed.

More traditional feminists wanted equality more than anything else from their political system. Movements that supported the Equal Rights Amendment, for example, were mainly staged as peaceful demonstrations that encouraged the need for the status of women to be officially equal in a nation dominated by a male government and power structure.

This hit the right note with many citizens. Such a struggle still continues, but it has been disrupted by calls by many more radical feminists to use any means possible, including violence, to disrupt a male-centric patriarchy that exists within the very fabric of our nation and all of its institutions.

Just to be clear, a patriarchy in America has existed since the nation's founding, but to replace such a patriarchy with a female-centric matriarchy will not sit well with many in this nation. Firstly, patriarchy itself may be a myth, considering how many women are now outpacing men in both education, employment, and industry. While things at the top of the food chain may seem bleak, the fact is that many women do dominate professions that are in the middle and are run exclusively by women. There are even some industries that are so exclusively female that men still have no access to them. An example of this is the more female traditional fields of nursing, teaching, and now writing and publishing, which are easily well-known to be female-dominated at the present. There are many other industries that are just as important and just as lucrative for women but to say that men dominate every industry and every form of government is really an exaggeration designed, not to uplift women to equal status, which is a positive effect, but to overtake and dominate men, just as any patriarchy does women. A woman's equality is one cause, but the cause for any woman to be the first among equals is quite another.

While there have been many advances in female achievement over the decades since women's suffrage, many feminists won't ever acknowledge that it is enough to achieve a simpler, much more achievable equality. Instead, it now becomes a question that leads many women to the idea of all-out warfare against a male-dominated society, which may be a total myth in the first place. The usual slew of *cause-celeb* exhortations, made by many prominent public figures who declare their growing discontent for men, doesn't help much and looks silly, because it happens all the time, in the same exact way, with every age. It's a media bandwagon.

What used to be a reasonable form of more traditional feminism has been replaced by something far more dangerous. It is the same system of thought that installed patriarchy as a system of dominance in the first place. The use of violence, then, to achieve some kind of social justice becomes the same weapon used over and over again, just like any other movement. Younger feminists are resorting to the same tactics, at least in theory and belief. Their thinking is similar to that of males who have dominated women in generations past.

Furthermore, if such a system of matriarchy came to dominate any space, a Utopian nation wouldn't inevitably result either. One can easily imagine a dystopia stemming from a matriarchy as well, no matter if it comes through violence or through the systematic dismantling of a prior patriarchal system.

For example, we can easily imagine a time in the future when females decide to separate completely from males due to their needs to maintain an equal status between men and women and form their own society. They protect their borders, almost like an all-female army does. Yet, females would still need men to reproduce.

This does not require physical sex anymore, but the union of female egg cells with male sperm cells developed in a petri dish in a lab somewhere in a neutral zone between the territory that divides the men and the women.

Who would determine whether or not that the result of each union is male or female? Who would determine where the greatest need for specialized genes in such a world is needed the most? Would a single woman decide? Would a democratic body of elders, both men and women, decide who gets exists and who does not? Would a female dictator take control and decide? What would happen to co-education? How would we define transgendered people? What process would be in place to determine the best system of government? Would it be an inclusive society if men can't join, and vice-versa? Are males and females who have been born and raised in the West be able to include women and men from other cultures as free and equal within their separate territories or within their own?

This is a just a simple example to illustrate the point that feminists, in general, have not developed their ideas of matriarchy enough to convince anyone that such a female-dominated system, whether within their own separate spaces or even within a collection of both men and women, will ever result in something that is better than the patriarchy that many feminists allege we have now. Feminists, then, have not utilized the tools of the imagination and creativity well enough to make their vision of matriarchy both feasible and reliable *as it directly relates to questions of political theory and the functions of government* at this time.

Certainly there has been much imagined about a matriarchy ever since the beginning of time, but as far as anything remotely feasible and reliable nothing has been advanced or projected within the realm of political science or political theory. Such creativity remains to be seen, which is why feminism, especially our Millennial adherents to whatever feminist ideologies they may now espouse, must first gain much more experience with traditional feminism that directed itself towards the fundamental need for equality that oppose the more radical approaches of violence, matriarchy, and separation that they now justify.

Final Thoughts on this Rumination

There are still some practical suggestions that we have to consider in order for our nation to emerge out of the horrors of our eighteen years of war that have exhausted both our resources and the lives of our servicemen and servicewomen. Is it then so wise to add to our national defense at this time and make investments in smart, more advanced technologies that defend our borders without providing enough medical care through the Veterans Administration and their fine network of hospitals and doctors when our long, arduous struggle as a nation in war has come to an end that is definitive, but in no way final? Should we fund our defense department, its industries, and its contractors, and not these same returning veterans, sick and injured as they are, who have fought this war?

If we do not support our returning soldiers fully enough by funding these hospitals that will inevitably have to integrate them into the civilian world, and instead add to our future technological defenses, whether this appropriation benefits us or not, we will never again trust a government or a defense department that drags us into a war that promises any kind of benefit when we cannot even uphold the very health of the people who had to nerve to serve our country in the first place. If returning veterans are not assisted medically, if it is not made a key and well-known policy, if the public senses that our government and our defense department has abandoned these returning soldiers in any kind of way and any such manner, as they definitely will, then the government and the defense department ought never to be trusted again with the lives of any recruit or anyone interested in the Armed Forces either.

Furthermore, and just to hammer the point home, the same goes for the entire military-industrial complex, which includes the factories, corporations, and the contractors-for-hire who simply circumvent the military in the pursuit of profit. If this complex, as gargantuan as it is, cannot serve veterans returning from the psychological and physical traumas that an eighteen-year foreign war that these veterans have fought, then an unforgiving public who will witness this return will definitely realize that such a complex does not serve their essential need to be protected and secure in order to survive either. Who would ever want to serve in such a military ever again? Who would want their prosecution?

And if the public senses this and no longer finds our military deserving of this essential trust to take care of its own wounded and sick, the public will end its service and support of the military and its industries in kind. The military-industrial complex, despite the best of its intentions in serving the needs of its soldiers, will be reduced to rubble and will be driven into the dirt as a result. The public will know that it has been tricked and duped once again into another deadly war. It is debatable whether or not the military-industrial complex even benefits the nation at this time. What we do know is that a backlash is sure to follow, and those who serve the military both in and around it, from the defense contractors to individually-armed missionaries, will feel the brunt of this backlash. There is little reason to invest in our future defenses at this time anyway with the exception of cybersecurity.

Veteran charities and the mysterious emergence of private-sector companies that offer benefits and services to returning veterans are simply just not enough nor should they ever be. What we need is immediate funding for the Veterans Administration and plenty of it to ensure the health and successful re-integration of our soldiers, yes, even our poorest ones into civilian life. A small scattering of non-profit support groups in a smattering of small towns and villages across the face of this enormous nation just won't do. Well-intentioned veterans' charities and fundraisers are simply not enough either. Support must be comprehensive and well-funded by our taxpayers who originally agreed to deploy troops to the Middle East in the first place. It must be made a national priority, and such a policy must be distributed hrough all mainstream media when it comes for our military service people to withdraw from the Middle East. This is but a suggestion, but it is also a strong and important one.

Secondly, as stated repeatedly in this rumination, there must be a re-evaluation of our binary system of government that has instilled within our minds and our hearts through countless generations these senseless zero-sum behaviors that are enforced by our Constitution, depending on which administration is elected to govern or which administration or which candidate in an election wins or loses. This means finding a way out of the two-party duopoly that will cripple the nation and will ultimately send it to ruin, no matter how many times we are permitted to switch sides, This has to be changed to a more plural form of power-sharing that represents not one winning section and one losing section, but an all-winning section at a reduced and acceptable level that everyone can live with. An empire has to end at some point if it can no longer adapt or change. The United States is no exception. We must learn to compromise and cooperate again through pluralism in our government system. Yes-or-no, winner-take-all decision-making just won't bail our great nation out of trouble this time without dire consequences for everyone involved. We are talking about the most powerful among us too. If we do not compromise and cooperate, and if this cooperation is somehow veiled or hidden from a blood-thirsty public, then this condition will worsen and lead to our nation's demise, maybe not right away, but definitely in the near future. Let's hope we are wrong in this prediction in all ways, shapes, and forms, no matter what benefits this well-intended rumination provides.

Compromise and cooperation, even among fierce political enemies or opponents, in a binary system such as ours can be achieved, if and only if we can *imagine* it. We need not imagine a total solution to a particular issue or problem all at once or right away. Merely a limp band-aid that covers it and provides some kind of relief to our most ghastly differences will do at this present moment.

For example, let's take our fierce binary debate over the question of illegal immigration. Would it not be better to propose that border states pay for their own border protection than to rely on blanket federal policies that enforce a one-size-fits-all solution for our border wall issue? States like Texas, Arizona, and New Mexico could use their own state funding to build their own border walls, should their people decide to do so, while Californians, who believe in accepting undocumented immigrants to live, work, and breathe freely in the spaces they share, can initiate and befriend other states in proximity that have the room, such as the border states of Texas, Arizona, and New Mexico. This border states or

Midwestern states will agree to resettle at least some of the overflow of immigrants. California can then exchange a service that the border state or Midwestern state needs. Again, this encourages cooperation and harmony among states that seem to be opponents and enemies on opposite sides of an issue.

This may not work at all. This may be impossible, yes. This may be a laughable and ludicrous proposal, yes. But it is a start, even for the simpleton and ignoramus in us all. This crude and impossible solution can at least be a beginning of what needs reform in our dysfunctional immigration system, and, therefore, the pebble in the pond of inescapable binarism that ripples the surface of governance that does not allow for any such plurality whatsoever.

Sending newly-arrived immigrants into sanctuary cities is a terrible solution. So is doing nothing about the problem that illegal immigration poses to the working poor living in these border states who can't survive when they must leave their present jobs due to undocumented illegal workers from Honduras who work for very low wages.

Compromise and cooperation must exist between polar opposites if we are to survive. This also means that polar opposites must sacrifice their fair share of support to more centrist candidates and viable third-party candidates who straddle the middle, not to ensure their own victory in an election year, but to ensure the very survival of our conflicted nation.

Compromise and cooperation with the best of intentions for the public good, as far as we can see it, is a version of love no matter how criminal we are forced to become or how coarse our bargaining skills have to be used against each other. And the fundamental problem of a rumination such as this is that we will never know if such compromise and cooperation can exist in the condition we find ourselves.

We can never prove if love even exists, and even if we do believe it exists, it can never be applied rationally to the study of politics or be implemented within even the best ideas that we have within our dysfunctional political process and our unique Constitution that has set this bomb of binarism on our doorstep. The citizens of our nation will always be forced to travel up the middle on that razor-thin, infinitesimal line to escape to a better life, no matter who we are or how hard we have worked. If our sacred Constitution needs to be amended to alleviate this growing dysfunction, then let's at least bring up the topic.

Furthermore, it would be presumptuous to argue that love is always of such a positive quality that it is able to mean all of what we have written here. It is quite clear that these elements of love's definition aren't the only definitions of love. What happened to the negative qualities of love? The pain of never winning a true love, the loss of a woman's child who must die within her womb, the death of beloved child by the hands of a terrible disease or the gun of a murderer? These are also the negative consequences of loving in a nation such as ours or any other nation for that matter. Because in any nation and within each individual, love can never be completely kind or beautiful. It can never be as perfect or beautiful as we ever imagine it. There isn't even enough of it available to feed a starving child or a group of tortured children within our own borders. Love, in other words, doesn't necessarily have to be so positive. It can hurtful and neglectful, and it can lead our lives to ruinous ends. Love is that dangerous a force. And so is its opposite, which is fear. These are the two dangerous binary motivations that drive our American decision-making. Even this entire essay is problematic and specious at best even though penned with the best of intentions. Ruminating on such a topic has its limits. We are still faced with the same problems as we have always faced, no matter how long we ruminate on how we can apply love to our most compelling social ills.

Because in this great democracy of ours, we can't simply sit under a tree and ruminate our days and nights away attempting to find solutions to all of our problems, especially on as questionable and as volatile a question, such as the existence of this concept known as "Love." There is simply no such possibility for even the most venerable and gifted political scientist in any college or university on the edge of his or her retirement to ruminate in such a manner that can be healthy or responsible.

This gifted political scientist, this woman or man, whomever he or she may be, is just a human being in this nation, just like any other. This professor may have labored hard, taught his college and university students well, penned amazing theories that have at least moved our nation that crucial step forward towards the betterment of the human condition, or so he or she believes. But now, it all must end.

The political scientist must suddenly teach that final last class to his or her children who are restlessly seated in the desks before him, or her, in the near-vacant classroom that has employed the nation's most brilliant academicians from long ago. And maybe he or she has been told by the best psychiatrists and psychologists and doctors that in this reality we just can't ruminate anymore, especially about senseless absurdities such as love in any practical, real, or reckless manner without imposing the same sickness of rumination that we are diagnosed with onto the students who must hear our pleas to consider it as a rational and healthy method to address our most pressing and perplexing political problems. Maybe in another, more imaginary world we can do this, but never in the reality of today. No one has that luxury, and for any political scientist, time is running out.

The range and depth of his or her thinking and the expanse of time needed to make decisions will always be a luxury in our forever-abrupt reality. Rumination must be a sickness that will one day require a cure to keep this gifted professor alive. Rumination will always end in the finality and conclusion of a simple question mark. After all, we should simply stay far away from it, thinks the political scientist, especially when it comes to a rumination on love in our present national condition. No one can even be sure if love belongs in any realm of politics whatsoever, no matter how long and hard we apply ourselves to theories about its existence, or especially, apply it to the raw and practical processes of theory-making. We are just not made that way. But maybe the political scientist is still unsure.

After years of thought on the subject of our democracy, this is what the old professor is left with. This venerable and wisest of theorists, this once child-prodigy now stumbles into his or her classroom to teach the final lesson to, what seems like, rows and columns of newborn infants who will eventually govern his country now that he has finished serving them well. Similarly, this same professor, man or woman, will have even more time to ruminate after watching the film *Cocoon* with elderly friends at the nursing home near this same college or university. Even though this old political scientist still has that final evening of his or her life to ruminate, it still leads to the same set of questions. Never answers.

This incredibly gifted soul still has to collect the plastic tray at the table nearby to eat the final meal of cottage cheese, lime Jell-O, and a small plastic cup of prune juice. But after the old professor finishes and retires to his room, he or she must ask a final question: is any theory sick if pondering over it leads to the same set of questions? Is it insane to ask these same questions over and over again? Is the theorist still sick if, in his or her last breath, concludes that a new branch of study must be the start of a new genre that investigates the writers and poets of political science fiction? Or is this man or woman sick if the end result of his or her rumination on the current condition that reality has now presented calls an answer that has to be made before his or her inevitable death? Did the theorist succeed at all, or did he or she simply waste precious time imagining an idea that really never existed in the first place?

No human being can ever know. No human being will ever know. No human being can ever judge this theorist either. But at least this old professor has made an attempt to move beyond the finite set of old questions and has embraced the unknown functioning and application of love in a nation that is always fighting with itself. It is the present condition of his nation, not the rumination he or she uses, nor the effort that it takes to ruminate, that ultimately exhausts and finally consumes this old professor's life.